Contents

Part I   Developing Your Political Intelligence

Part II   Analyzing Political Styles

Part III   Staying on an Ethical Course in Politically Charged Situations

Part IV   Pulling It All Together

Preface

"**I** hate politics," comes the refrain of almost every public and nonprofit manager we know. "If only we didn't have to deal with politics, but just could deal with things rationally, then this job would be much easier." But we can't; nor should we want to.

WE CAN'T

Let's begin with a definition of organizational politics. It is "the use of power toward and through other people in an environment inside and outside the organization." You cannot help dealing with people. They are a necessary challenge and joy of managing any organization. People are the fundamental building blocks of an organization. They are one of the two major dimensions that Blake and Mouton talk about in their Managerial Grid and which are highlighted in the Ohio State studies (Blake and Mouton, 1964; Stodgil, 1974). People are everything, and politics is everywhere.

Pfeffer has emphasized that power is pervasive throughout the environment of an organization (1981). You can't help dealing with it. Power and politics invade your decision-making patterns; they affect your interpersonal decisions with those above you and those below you; they pervade your seeking of resources and spending of them. You can't help but deal with politics. It is ubiquitous. It is as present as the air we breathe.

NOR SHOULD YOU

Politics is power. You can have no effect without power. You can't win a trial if you're a powerless attorney. You can't teach your students if you're a powerless teacher, and you can't be a good leader if you're powerless to make things happen in your organization. All professions need power and must ensure the use of that power to good ends.

French and Raven (1959) discuss the sources of power, such as position in the organization, expertise, and personal charisma. Whatever your source of power, be prepared to amass it and use it—for good ends. We know that the idea of amassing power may run counter to some managers' and leaders' ideals, but unless you become adept at power, you and your organization will soon be left behind or fall into the hands of those who are adept and whose goals may not be compatible with your own. Politics gives you power. Politics hones your power so that you can bring your organization to noble ends.

TARGET AUDIENCE

While there are many books written about politics in the private sector, the political challenges in the public sector are vastly different. Educational leaders at all levels face the intense political conflicts that arise in this age of increasing expectations and diminishing resources. The fact that everything we do is subject to public scrutiny dramatically escalates the consequences of error in this arena. Those consequences can severely affect the organization's standing and future, and they can also severely affect the leader's standing and future.

Leaders are practical. Politics are practical. This is first and foremost a practical book. It is written to be useful to busy leaders and managers of public schools, higher education, and nonprofit organizations who are trying desperately to keep all the plates spinning and, at the same time, are grappling with political situations for which they are largely unprepared. They need help, and they need it now!

For that reason, it is written in simple English, chock full of stories that each of us has experienced in our long careers. It is written without a lot of theoretical gibberish or obtuse meanings. It is written to be used tomorrow, and tomorrow and tomorrow, as a guide to political activity. It is written to help you become a more powerful leader, one who is respected for the ability to deliver the dream for the organization. It is written to help you prevent political traumas. And it is written to help you find your way out of political catastrophes. Following the suggestions in this book will help you to become a more politically intelligent leader—one with the courage and know-how to tackle those daily dilemmas and major issues in the high-stakes political environment that characterizes our world today.

ORGANIZATION OF THE BOOK

We have divided this book into three sections: politics, politics, and politics!

Part I deals with nineteen political strategies to help you manage the external environment and eighteen political strategies you might use to manage the internal environment of the organization. You will learn how to build your power base and become more influential in determining the destiny of your organization by working with people inside and outside the system.

Part II deals with the political styles you might manifest in your working relationships. Through an instrument we have developed, you will be able to identify the primary, secondary, and tertiary political styles that you use in practice. It will also help you to identify the styles that others use and give you some suggestions on which strategies are most influential with people who exhibit the characteristics of those styles.

Part III discusses the ethics of politics. It describes political elements of ethical dilemmas and offers suggestions on dealing with highly charged situations and special interest groups associated with public sector leadership. These groups include public sector unions, elected boards and councils, volunteers, advisory groups, and foundations.

In part IV, we provide some scenarios to give you practice in using all of the strategies and ideas set forth in this book.

Looking for a recipe book that will protect you from politics and the personal stress that comes with it? There are no exact recipes or formulas for that. What we've tried to come up with is a resource that (1) assures leaders that politics are normal, (2) tells them something about their own political style, (3) builds political competency with tried and true strategies, and

(4) offers guidance on how to stay the course ethically even when the political chips are down.

PREMISES

There are five premises to this book:

1. All Politics Are Local

While state, federal, and international politics have much meaning for each of us, especially relative to security, local politics are where we live our lives. Whether it is schooling for our children, the streets we drive on, the houses we build, the partnerships we form, or day-to-day management of our organizations, we use local politics and local strategies. We seek to affect government decisions and citizen preferences to our way of thinking. We seek to form alliances with other organizations and to persuade those in our institution to go along with us.

Decisions at every level are made based on how it affects us locally in the smallest microcosm of any organization. Understanding the local impact of any proposal is what creates breakthrough political solutions. All politics are local. Believe it.

2. There Are Multiple and Splintered Groups Out There

Ever hear, "Everybody thinks this!" No! No! No! Everybody does not think this. Within any organization, there are multiple groups with differing opinions. Even within a small group, there often are diverse opinions. You've got to know the landscape of thought out there and strategize accordingly.

I remember when we tried as a city council to build a third fire station; the neighbors complained and said, "Nobody wants it." With a little investigation, we found that only a few of the neighbors didn't want the fire station. The rest of the city wanted it, and even within the neighborhood there were pockets of opinions that were for it. But if we had listened to the neighbors who testified at the city council, we wouldn't have built the third fire station. There are multiple and splintered groups out there. Your job is to find them!

3. Politics Start Off Where Rationality Leaves Off

We said earlier that most leaders and managers yearn for a rational world. However, Pfeffer (1981) says three conditions allow rationality to work: (1) plentiful resources, (2) no ambiguity of goals, and (3) no conflict over priorities. Nutt, in different words, affirms the same thing (1960). In the public sector, it is very rare that we would have even one of these conditions, never mind all three.

Rationality may be devoutly desired, but rarely does it work to the fullest degree. We have to remember that politics enters into almost all issues, even when we do have a moderate degree of rationality. Politics is at the intersection of conflict, uncertainty, and managing people. And that's where most of us live. Don't expect rational behavior in politically turbulent situations.

4. Behaviors Are Important

You can control behaviors; you can change behaviors. That is why the strategies contained in this book are presented in terms of what you do, not what you think. Attitudes are important, but they change as a result of behavioral changes. You can hate politics, but as long as you act in a politically astute fashion, you will change that attitude eventually. Behavioral changes precede attitudinal ones. Politics are here to stay—learn to deal with it. Better still, learn to be good at it!

5. Simple Strategies

Politics can best be learned by going from the simple to the complex. You can't learn by going from the complex to the simple. That is why we present the strategies contained in this book in a simple, straightforward way, rather than dwelling on complex theories of power and influence. This book is meant to be practical. Political events erupt because simple step-by-step strategies are not used early on in the process. This book gives you the strategies to head off disaster, to positively influence outcomes, and to stay in an ethical decision-making mode. We will also help you learn how to use them effectively.

These five premises provide the overarching framework for this book.

VOICE

One last thing needs to be said about the voice we use. We will tell stories in the first person, either "I" or "we." This may mean "I, Pat" or "I, Tom" or "I, Larry." It doesn't matter to us, nor should it to the reader. Not all of the stories are our own. Some are the stories of colleagues that we have observed as they engaged in their own struggles with political situations. What matters is the story and the point it serves.

Acknowledgments

The authors wish to give special recognition to the University of La Verne doctoral students in organizational leadership. Their participation in our political seminars, their involvement in our field projects, and their use of our materials have contributed to a richer development of this book on organizational politics. It is our hope that their political intelligence will help them to successfully deliver a noble vision for their organizations.

1

DEVELOPING YOUR POLITICAL INTELLIGENCE

1

The Politically Intelligent Leader Defined

As we said in the preface to this book, politics is "the use of power toward and through other people in an environment inside or outside the organization." Let us expand on this definition. It is the unintentional and intentional activities, strategies, or tactics that you use to lead people to your point of view. It can be for individual benefit or organizational benefit. It can be for good ends or not-so-good ends, depending on the ethics of your views. This book is dedicated to helping you achieve moral ends in a public sector organizational setting—namely the education arena.

Of course we all hear daily about politics at local, state, national, and international levels. Sometimes, we're able to see how political strategies used effectively can bring peace to nations on the brink of war, or help to get a bill passed for humanitarian aid. But more often than not, we hear about political shenanigans and corrupt politicians. This is what gives politics a bad name and leaves many with the feeling that politics is inherently unethical—a view we hope to change.

Local politics, as defined here, includes strategies used internally in an organization or externally in a local community to effect some action on behalf of the people.

The strategies you use will either attract supporters to your point of view or lose them to another direction. If you lack the power to translate ideas and beliefs into action, you will not be an effective leader. You need political intelligence if you are to become a powerful leader in today's competitive environment. What do we mean by the term "politically intelligent leader"?

The politically intelligent leader is one who uses a moral compass to lead the organization in the right direction while considering the wants, needs, values, motivations, and emotions of followers and stakeholders.

This book is dedicated to helping you become a politically intelligent leader—the effective and ethical leader your organization and your people need. What goes into becoming a politically intelligent leader? Let's take a look.

INTERNAL POLITICS

When you are trying to create a change within an organization, you are dealing with internal local politics. When you are trying to resolve a human conflict within an organization, you are dealing with local politics. When you are trying to convince your board to decide on a course of action, or when you are building a team or planning your budget, you are dealing with local politics. In these and so many other ways, you are strategizing to bring people to a point of view that you support. The politically intelligent leader needs an understanding of the internal territory—the key players, the issues, the culture, the potential blind spots, and the strategies that tend to be persuasive in galvanizing people to constructive action.

EXTERNAL POLITICS

External politics are just that—outside the organizational setting. They are the realm of networking and power relationships. They are more obvious than internal politics but are nonetheless difficult to perform skillfully.

When you are leading a boundary committee for a school district, you are dealing with external local politics. When you are planning the placement of a park site, you are dealing with local politics. When you are proposing a rate hike in utility costs, or the closing of a school, you are dealing with local politics. In these and countless other ways, you need to employ appropriate strategies to get the job done.

There are no exact formulas—no recipe books of strategies. The politically intelligent leader must pick and choose strategies that will work with specific types of people in particular situations. While some strategies are more universally appropriate than other ones, the leader must choose. In the chapters to follow, we will provide a menu of alternative strategies. They are intentional strategies that a politically intelligent leader must consciously select for deployment in a particular situation.

POLITICAL MYTHS

There are three prevailing myths in the realm of organizational politics that are particularly hard to dispel:

1. The first is that decision making is rational. It's not! Pfeffer (1981) describes decision making as rational when the following conditions are present:

   a. resources are plentiful,
   b. goals are unambiguous and consistent, and
   c. there is no conflict over priorities.

   Seldom is even one of these conditions present, let alone all three! In most public sector organizations, resources are scarce, but goals are plentiful and diverse. Setting priorities is frequently riddled with conflict because there's immense competition for resources. But somehow we continue to assume that decision making is nonetheless logical, factual, and data driven. Alas, it is not. It is full of power influences, and the use of power is another name for politics. Assume that decision making is not rational and, on occasion, you might be pleasantly surprised.

2. The second myth is that politics will go away. We'd like to assume that if we just close our eyes for a time that "bad" things will go away. But they never do. The same is true with politics. You have to deal with it, no matter how distasteful it may be to you. If you don't, politics will come back to haunt you in "bigger and badder" ways. Politics is like conflicts. If you catch them while they're small, they are manageable. But if you avoid them and let them fester, they can escalate, potentially spinning dangerously out of control. If you

manage political situations while they are small, you can control them and direct them. Later you may not be able to.

3. Politics is easy. We assume that if we take a simple and direct strategy, such as just telling people of our decisions, that will do it. It seldom does. Politics is complex. It requires insight, analysis, and careful handling.

While the strategies in this book are stated in noncomplex ways, they are complicated to perform. They are far from easy. Most situations require the insight and the will to use them. They require preplanning and time. To become a politically intelligent leader requires five things:

a. knowing and analyzing the situation at hand;
b. knowing strategies and applying the right ones;
c. readjusting the strategies that miss their mark;
d. using a moral compass to guide you in politically turbulent times; and
e. knowing that no matter how good you are, sometimes things don't work out, and you need some special strategies to help you through those tough times.

POLITICS CAN BE SATISFYING

Politics is neither bad nor good—it simply is. Developing your political intelligence quotient—your PIQ—can indeed be satisfying because it gives you the power to further your organization's goals and values.

Lest you think that politics is inherently unethical, read on to chapter 6. There you will learn more about how to keep ethics alive and maintain your integrity as you are making those politically volatile decisions.

Politics and power are rampant in and around all kinds of institutions. For the survival of both you and your organization, you need to be skilled in understanding your own and others' political styles and potential strategies, at the very least, and find them satisfying as a tool to achieve noble ends, at the very best.

FINAL THOUGHTS

In this day and age, you have to be fast on your feet. Sometimes the situation changes; sometimes the actors change; sometimes the result changes. Situations are complex and require knowledge of both internal and external strategies. This is why it's critical for the politically intelligent leader to know as many strategies as possible and be prepared to use them when the situation warrants.

2

External Strategies

I remember many years ago, when I was younger and more naive, I wanted to tear down an unused school site and build a commercial development. As superintendent, I had surveyed all the parents, and they did not object for the most part. So I made a proposal to the board. Well, the nonparent community around the school came apart at the seams. They were adamantly against any venture that would disturb their serene neighborhood. Also, one of the few parents who were against my proposal was the editor of the local newspaper. I had failed to use the strategies that I propose in this book. The protest became so loud that I had to abandon the idea. The board was in full flight.

This is just one of the stories we could tell about our failure to fully take into account external politics. We hope you can learn from our mistakes as well as our successes.

Leaders of public and nonprofit organizations have multiple constituencies who have an interest, or perceived interest, in the business of your enterprise. Whether you like it or not, the politically intelligent leader has to deal in external politics, that is, those politics that involve groups outside of your organization. Becoming mindful of these constituencies is the first step in honing your political skills.

Through our experience and research, we have developed nineteen strategies that we think will help you cope with groups and individuals external to your agency. This is not an exhaustive list but rather some suggestions that we consider to be extremely useful and practical. You may want to add others. Not all of the strategies that we suggest are applicable to every situation. Developing your own insights and intuitions about which tools to use when comes from practice and a heightened level of consciousness, both of which we hope you will have after reading this book.

THE NINETEEN EXTERNAL STRATEGIES

1. Build Trust

The most important and universally needed strategy is to build trust—whether it is with external or internal constituencies. Building trust, however, is not just saying "trust me" or expecting trust because of your position in the organization, your personal charisma, or your reputation. You build trust with your behaviors—the things you do. Trust, in fact, is made up of five behaviors, as presented in *Building Teams, Building People* (Harvey and Drolet, 2004, pp. 21–24):

Interdependence

When I need you and you need me, we have a basis for trust. When I need you but you do *not* need me, you can be arbitrary and capricious and at some point probably will be. The reverse is equally true. Only when we have mutual need can trust evolve.

Think of the phrase often spoken between couples, "You take me for granted." This is simply another way of saying, "You don't demonstrate your need for me." A task sociogram is one way of assessing this condition in an organizational setting. Working with a group of five to ten, ask everyone, "Who do you need to get your job done?" Then look for mutual two-way transactions—pairs of people who say they need each other. The more two-way transactions in a group, the higher the capacity for trust will be. The more one-way transactions, the lower the probability of trust. The more we need each other, both in reality and in perception, the more we can build trust. To build trust, you need to determine how you can fill a need that others may have rather than only looking to them to fill your needs. You can develop your own sensitivity to their needs through observation and good listening skills.

Consistency

Research shows that people trust those who are consistent from word to deed and from deed to deed. Of these two, the former is most important—"I can count on you to do what you say." In a colloquial phrase, you "walk the talk." Much disillusionment with politicians reflects their inconsistency between word and deed. In the battle to win, politicians promise much, but in the face of reality, they deliver little. They talk about cutting back and then give themselves pay raises.

Contrast such politicians with one of our small-business clients facing the recession of Christmas 1990. This businessman told his employees there would be reductions and cutbacks—and he started by cutting his own salary 25 percent and dropping all his club memberships. Those actions sent a message that he was serious and could be trusted to experience the same shortfalls as everyone else. Later, when business improved, he did not restore his benefits until everyone else's benefits were in place. He modeled what he asked of others.

Other examples are university deans who talk of academic priorities and then teach regularly to show their commitment, or elementary school principals who are regularly visible on the playground, at the bus stop, and in classrooms. Behavior needs to be consistent with verbal priorities. When you act in ways that say your words can be trusted, you enrich the entire climate of the organization.

Honesty

People who lie, cheat, and double deal are simply not trusted. You can get away with these behaviors in the short run, but in the long run, duplicitous actions become widely known. You cannot hide this kind of light under a basket. Dishonesty can involve both commission and omission. Telling lies is not the only form of dishonesty; forgetting to mention the truth is also dishonest. When you are known to be honest and committed to integrity, you build trust.

Affability

Likable people are easier to trust. Affability supports trusting relationships. To be likable is not sufficient, however, although some leaders foolishly try to build trust solely on that basis. The manager who walks around being "one of the group" but is without substance may be well liked but is not apt to be trusted on the professional level necessary to build effective teams.

Likewise, colleagues or managers who persistently express negative attitudes and whine about everything are hard to relate to. I once worked for a university president who whined and moaned about all the catastrophes about to befall us. In the process, he was trying to set himself up as the university's savior. All he accomplished was to make himself the least-liked and least-trusted person on campus. Affability, though only fourth on this list, does still contribute to trusting, positive relationships.

Extension of Trust

There is an old but true aphorism that says, "Those who give trust get trust." When you send messages to colleagues that you will give trust only when they "deserve" it, you set up cautious and untrusting relationships. No, this is not a Pollyanna world in which everyone is loving and nice. When you extend trust, you may well be violated. You need to anticipate such eventualities and think through in your own mind what you will do when they occur. But if you avoid extending trust for fear of violation, you will then be a double victim—they will have achieved their purpose and you will have gained nothing at all. Your fear of giving trust will make you a less-trusted person. Remember: the messages you send are the messages you receive—those who give trust, get trust.

When these five conditions—interdependence, consistency, honesty, affability, and extension of trust—are present, the soil is fertile for trust. This equation is not perfectly predictive, but the probability is high that when these five conditions exist, trust does also. With trust, you have a richer organizational climate.

I remember a case when I first was elected to a city council in 1984. I ran on the platform of mobile home rent control and was elected. I established a committee in which both sides felt needed—the park owners and the residents. I gave all the information to everyone, and I acted in a consistent, honest manner. We crafted a proposal that met the needs of both sides. It was quickly passed by the council, and it still stands today. I established mutual trust with what were then warring factions. Since then, I have been reelected five times. If you act in a trustworthy fashion, they will too.

2. Create a Political Vision

In turbulent times, where goals are ambiguous, resources are scarce, and there is conflict over priorities, the situation is ripe for political blunders. A leader who parachutes into a crisis without a compass is likely to get lost and may not survive.

A clear political vision provides a beacon and a compass to guide you through those potential disasters. It clarifies your identity in your own mind and gives you confidence in your direction. It helps you to organize your actions and resources around your values and priorities. It facilitates strategic thinking and minimizes confusion in your own mind and in your communications with others.

Your political vision is based on both insight and foresight. As Irene Sanders says in *Strategic Thinking and the New Science*, "Whatever is happening today is shaping tomorrow" (1998, p. 110). You need to develop insights about what's happening in the world around you right now in order to be able to project what could happen and what should happen in the future. You also need to develop self-awareness to understand how your own aspirations, anxieties, and actions can influence the foresight you have for the future.

To develop a political vision, answer the following questions as they relate to you and your organization:

1. What are your core beliefs and values?
2. What are the organizational strengths that should be valued and maintained?
3. What are the long-term goals and priorities for your organization, yourself, and your relationships?
4. What is happening now internally and externally that can give you insights about the future?
5. What are the connections, patterns, and interrelationships that can help or hinder your long-term goals?

Your political vision helps you to focus on the "whole" rather than individual parts—which is critical to political and leadership effectiveness.

For example, concentrating on a specific change that you feel is needed, and sacrificing relationships to achieve it, can win the battle but lose the war in delivering the overall vision.

Your political vision also helps you to maintain your own values and beliefs when chaos might tempt you to compromise ethics in negotiating an agreement. It helps you to be clear about your priorities when your personal survival may be at risk. And it helps you to influence outcomes without manipulating people with hidden agendas and unethical tactics.

One of my mentors gave me this advice when I was a fledgling administrator. He said, "Pick the hills to die on. You can't go to the wall on everything or you lose your ability to accomplish anything." He was pointing me toward the importance of values-based priorities—a key element of political vision.

Use the worksheet in figure 2.1 to help you develop your own political vision that can guide your long-term and short-term choices and decisions.

3. You Need to Meet Their Needs or They'll Never Meet Yours

If you wait until you need someone and then try to meet his or her needs as an incentive to support you, you'll be too late. They will feel manipulated and used, and they surely will not meet your needs. I remember a neighboring city manager who waited until he needed senior citizens to pass a bond issue. He courted them and promised them the world. But they didn't trust him. He needed their vote, and they weren't going to give it to him. They overwhelmingly voted down the bond issue, and it failed by five percentage points. Alas, he didn't learn his lesson and went out again without meeting their needs first. Again he lost. The city manager should have tended to their needs and wants, and when they were satisfied and trusted that he was going to deliver what he had promised, they would meet his. Their needs come first. As a superintendent friend likes to point out, "You need to make a lot of deposits before you make a withdrawal."

4. Simplify and Clarify Your Message

It is important to convey the message you want to send in simple, straightforward terms. If you want your followers to understand your message and follow it, you must make it simple and avoid "rabbit runs." In the

Core Beliefs and Values

Organizational Strengths to Be Maintained

Current Internal and External Developments That Give Insights about the Future

Internal	External

Long-Term Goals and Priorities

Yourself	Your Organization	Your Relationships

Connections, Patterns, and Interrelationships That Can Help or Hinder Goals

Connections	Patterns of Relationships	Interrelationships (Networks, Coalitions)

Figure 2.1   Political Vision Worksheet

South, hunters on a raccoon hunt often take their dogs. The dogs would get the scent of a raccoon and chase it. But if a rabbit would cross the raccoon path, the dogs would get distracted and change their course to go after the rabbit. The hunters would then have to yank the dogs back to their original scent. Don't get distracted by miscellaneous issues that may get in the way of the message you want and need to communicate. Don't let rabbit runs derail your message.

Simplicity wins, complexity loses. Too many leaders make their messages complex and full of jargon. To give you an example of what we are talking about, a poor message might be the following:

> Pursuant to the goal of attaining maximum results on state-adopted standardized assessments, it is imperative to be cognizant of the fact that ECE programs initiated prior to commencing kindergarten have been invaluable in ameliorating underachievement and have served as a causal factor in enhanced academic performance of adolescents in elementary and secondary schools.

On the other hand, translating this into a good, simple message, it might sound like this:

> Preschool programs have a strong record of improving student test scores all the way through high school.

5. Never Let 'Em See You Sweat

Conflict frequently brings out the worst in people. The prospect of unbridled emotion—anger, hostility, and rage—can summon fear and anxiety in the hearts of even the most experienced leaders. This is especially true if the conflict takes place in a public setting or with an audience of any kind. However, any display of fear can invite an even more aggressive and prolonged attack by political opponents.

If you are worried, nervous, or fearful, there is a greater tendency to frown, squint, squirm, or sweat. Your breathing is shallow, your mouth is dry, and you find it harder to speak smoothly and fluently. You may not say enough, you might say too much, or you might say the wrong thing and incite the group further.

What can you do about it? Anticipating the situation is helpful. Understanding who will be attending the meeting, what their issues are,

and who will be speaking, if it is a formal meeting, helps you to prepare yourself.

Developing a plan for the encounter could include the development
of ground rules for conducting the meeting, which should be shared
with everyone at the beginning of the agenda. Later is too late. If you
find yourself in a toxic organization, it may be wise to start each meeting with a cordial welcome, followed by ground rules read in a neutral,
professional tone. In this way, "heated" visitors do not take the ground
rules as personally as if you were to wait until their item comes up on
the agenda. For example, board meetings may include norms like time
limits for speakers, alternating speakers for and against the proposal,
nontransfer of remaining time to other speakers, and the total time
available for public input on the entire item.

If you expect an emotionally charged confrontation at the meeting, you
should prepare yourself and colleagues ahead of the meeting with guidelines for handling the inevitable personal attacks and misinformation.
Your plan should consider psychological preparedness—steeling yourself for unkind words and hostility, for heart-wrenching sad stories, or for
sympathetic figures or local heroes brought in to speak in favor of the opposition. For example, parents may bring their young children in to play
their instruments at a board meeting when the school board is considering a financial cut to the music program that will help balance next year's
budget. Or a war hero might return to speak in favor of a coach whose
contract is about to be terminated. Or the parents of a child whose frag-
ile medical condition needs extraordinary nursing services on a daily basis may come to oppose cuts in the nursing program. It's hard not to feel
like the "hard-hearted villain" when making recommendations for the organization's financial security in face of human stories like the above.
You and your staff and your decision makers need to think through these
possibilities ahead of time in order to be at your best during these sensitive meetings.

You should consider ahead of time the options for follow-up that you
can announce after public input. For example, you might let the attendees
at a school board meeting know that you will be taking up these items
with the District Budget Committee or that your staff will investigate their
concerns. Or you might just close the public discussion, take the matter
under advisement, and schedule it for action at the next meeting. Or you

might decide to move ahead with board discussion, at which time the board may explain their views and then take action.

During the meeting, your body language needs to demonstrate that you are professional, confident, and willing to listen but intolerant of abuse. Visualizing yourself in the situation ahead of time will help to achieve the right balance. Take deep breaths before beginning the meeting. It helps to put enough air in your lungs to give your voice strength and fluency, and it calms you down.

Your facial expression needs to be open, pleasant, and relaxed. Make steady eye contact with those who are speaking, even if they are assaulting you. Looking down, to the side, or over their heads suggests that you are guilty, disinterested, or arrogant. People read frowns as disagreement or disapproval.

Attacking a pleasant, professional, sincere person tends to make rude, aggressive attackers look like bullies and makes reasonable people back away from them as their spokespersons. Taking notes during the speeches can help you to get through the attacks, stay more objective, and have a record of ideas to follow up on after the meeting. It also lets them know that you are taking their ideas seriously.

Resist the temptation to argue with the speakers or to return the attack with one of your own. Let them vent even if it becomes redundant. Listen and respond briefly to correct any misinformation when they are finished. At the end, share your next steps to consider their concerns.

6. Do Your Homework

Walking into a situation without good information is like walking blindfolded through a minefield. In order to avoid potential explosions and plan a course of action, you need to gather data from a variety of sources about

- the key issues at hand,
- groups that have influence in your community,
- powerful individuals that may have an interest in this issue,
- individuals who stand apart from the group,
- who is connected with whom in the circle of decision makers,
- what points are persuasive with key groups and individuals, and
- the "hot buttons" that ignite involved groups or individuals.

Knowing who is likely to be for a proposal or opposed to it helps you to identify the persuasive points and the hot buttons for each group. Knowing who the independent thinkers are might suggest people who will be willing to listen to your proposal and give it fair consideration. They may be able to help influence others who are not as yet involved in the controversy.

It's vitally important to understand the connections that might exist between opinion makers. Sometimes these lie below the surface and are not well known to others. For example, a decision maker's wife may be in a bridge club with another woman in the group of activists. Others may go to the same church. These informal lines of communication tend to be extremely influential in controversial decisions. Understanding how they might play a part in shifting the power from one side to the other is crucial.

Once you know the likely dynamics, it is important to identify what will be persuasive with these individuals and what the potential hot buttons are that could send them over to the opposition.

For example, if you want to build support for a bond election, persuasive points might include developing a list of improvements so that every neighborhood school has something to gain from supporting passage, rather than just two or three schools. A hot button might include using the bond to build a school in a new affluent neighborhood while closing a school in an older neighborhood.

Use a variety of techniques to gather data. Conferring with trusted associates who have insights about people and issues, attending meetings of various power groups, and having "coffees" to share information and listen to people talk and ask questions all help to discover important information about how people will react to your proposal and what they might find persuasive or incendiary. Reading local newspapers, editorials, and letters to the editor, as well as homeowner association newsletters tells you who is concerned about what. And it helps you to learn about the culture in your environment. Sometimes holding focus groups or surveying the constituents can also elicit helpful information about potential issues. The main idea here is, ask questions, ask questions, ask questions!

When you have the right data, but not before, you can determine a strategy that will work. Also keep in mind that circumstances change, so you need to do this kind of environmental scanning recurrently. Doing it once won't work, since every situation is different. One new person in the group or one new issue creates a whole new dynamic.

<u>Date</u> _____

Key Issues of This Situation:

Influential Groups	Influential Individuals	Independent Thinkers	Connections That Could Help	Connections That Could Hurt

Persuasive Points *(arguments or actions that will garner support)*	Hot Buttons *(what to avoid saying or doing)*

Figure 2.2   Political Homework Worksheet

Using the political homework worksheet in figure 2.2 will help you to cover all your bases as you plan your own strategy for handling a political hot fire.

7. Know Each Decision Maker's Agenda

Before you introduce a change initiative, it's wise to have information about how various stakeholders and decision makers will react to it. Those who have a stake in the outcome of a project have the potential to be allies or resistors. They will view a proposed initiative from their own perspective and consider how it will affect their own personal goals. Therefore, your success depends on knowing a great deal about the goals of your stakeholders and decision makers. To the extent that you can demonstrate how your initiative advances one of their causes, you have a much better chance of gaining their support.

But how do you find out what might be in their hidden agenda? Observe and reflect. Notice the following:

- What do they talk about in meetings and informal gatherings?
- How did they react to other initiatives that were proposed?
- What concerns do they raise in discussions of new ideas?
- How do they spend their time, and with whom?

Gathering this information with subtlety, over time, will help you to plan your approach. Knowing their concerns helps you to identify ways to address them as part of your proposal. Knowing who they spend time with helps you to ascertain who is influential with them. Understanding their goals helps you to create approaches that will help them to achieve their goals through support for your initiative. In this way, you can co-opt the opposition and possibly even create an ally.

8. Be Aware of Political Blind Spots

Joel De Luca defines the political blind spot as "not consciously seeing the extent to which informal influence shapes the decision making process" (1999, p. 27). Every situation presents the opportunity for political blind spots—those factors that are not obvious at first glance but can affect what you are trying to accomplish. Unknown relationships between opponents and decision makers, concealed goals, political favors, secret coalitions—all may become political blind spots that can come back to hurt you. It's particularly difficult to be aware of all the potential blind spots in the external environment of your organization.

On one occasion, there was a school district that was trying to raise the school use fees to cover utilities, repairs and replacement of classroom furniture, and carpeting. The heavy use by outside groups had generated increased costs from wear and tear, and the budget was tight, as usual. The district needed more revenue for its maintenance budget. It seemed like a simple matter to announce the change in fees to users for the next school year. However, one of the heaviest users was an organization whose CEO had close ties with a city council member. The council member called school board members to complain about the fee increase. He also went to the newspapers and used the council meeting to complain about this lack of district support for important public service groups in the community. This political blind spot cost the district negative press and many hours of meetings with city government representatives and facility users before resolution.

There were several blind spots. One was the fact that a facility user who had received positive support from the school district and many years of very reasonable use of a public facility would take such political measures about a rate increase, since their costs could be passed on to their consumers. Another blind spot was the connection between the CEO of the user group and a city council member. The third blind spot was that a city council member would initiate political action against another public agency that was outside the realm of his oversight.

Exposing your political blind spots may not be easy, and you can't do it alone. You need the help of people you trust to figure out where they might exist. Taking the time to develop awareness that those blind spots are out there is a big step forward. It helps you to think about relationships that could affect your goal success. With the help of others, you may secure enough information to discover many of those little-known connections before you get blindsided in the public decision-making arena.

9. Coalition Building Is a Long-Term and Necessary Strategy

Coalition building is a powerful strategy for external politics. It means forming a temporary alliance to get something accomplished. The "something" might be the passing of a bond issue, legislation on abused children, enforcement of border controls, or a new energy policy. Whatever the issue might be, the coalition comes together for some important purpose. This will not happen in a short time. It will only be brought about by doing the following:

1. identifying the issue of import,
2. forming a key group of those that already support the issue,
3. establishing the urgency behind the issue,
3. maintaining intermittent rewards for those who make incremental steps toward accomplishing the goal, and
4. gathering a wider group of influential backers.

In this way, you can build your coalitions over time so that when you need your allies, they are ready to support you.

10. "Working the Community" Is Usually neither Interesting nor Fun, but It's Necessary

It's not fun to spend your evenings after a long workday going to countless blue and gold Cub Scout dinners. It's not fun going to the Chamber mixers when your family is home waiting for you to come to dinner. It's not fun going to retirement dinners, especially if you hardly know the person. It's not fun going to the Kiwanis breakfast when you were out late the night before to attend a city council meeting. But it is important work. For everything you go to, you say with your presence that you honor the recipients and care for them.

You can't hope that someone will attend your functions, coalition meetings, or planning retreats if you don't attend theirs. It is time consuming, and you never know what yields the most "bang" for attendance. But you go anyway—that is, if you're politically astute.

11. Don't Wait to Build Networks till You Need Them

This is a corollary to strategy number 3. You cannot wait until you need networks to build them. I remember a public service agent for an electric company. She did everything she could to connect with her clients and help the cities in her territory. She was there to facilitate installations; she waived service charges where it was a hardship; she participated in civic committees; she did it all. Then, after five years, the electric company had an energy crisis and she needed to have legislation passed. She got it passed in the "blink of an eye." Her networking had been successful. The time she had spent had not gone unnoticed.

She had persevered with the strategy that said, "You don't build networks when you need them." She had spent five years cultivating hers, and it paid off. So, too, you must cultivate your networks long before you need them.

12. Include All Sides

There is an old adage that goes, "Keep your friends close; keep your enemies even closer." It is easy to form a committee that includes your supporters. It's harder to include your resistors. But you must deal with them sometime, and you might as well cope with them in committee when you can determine the power of their ideas while your proposal is in the formative stage. This gives you the opportunity to have the kind of dialogue that lets both of you consider possible modifications that might be warranted and useful in reaching agreement.

In the example used earlier about the rent control conflict, I included the residents of the parks on the committee. This was soundly applauded. I then included all the park owners. This was met with many groans. But I persevered, and in three months we had an ordinance. This ordinance has persisted for over twenty years and has been highly successful. This success came from the strategy to include all sides. They hammered out the issues and came to resolution. If I had put together a committee representing only one side of the issues, then the ordinance would have been a failure if it had been passed at all. It pays to include all sides.

13. Positive Responses to Perceived Dangers Win Support

Leading people is risky business. Proposing change threatens comfort, security, and success and causes the threatened to strike out at the leader. "When fears and passions run high, people can become desperate as they look to authorities for the answers. This dynamic renders adaptive contexts inherently dangerous" (Heifetz and Linsky, 2002, p. 14). How you respond to their verbal assault and psychological battering can have a great impact on the survival of the change, the organization, and you as their leader.

The CEO of a nonprofit foundation proposed some changes in the list of programs they had been sponsoring for many years. Times had changed. Needs were different. New programs had emerged that seemed to be a higher priority. The veteran members on the foundation board were outraged. Representatives of the existing programs were furious, as they saw their resources shifting to other programs. They demanded a public meeting. Although the CEO cringed at the thought of facing an angry mob, he stepped up to the plate. He scheduled the meeting, listened open-mindedly to the concerns, and promised to work with a committee of stakeholders to develop a solution they could bring back to the board that would consider their issues as well as the emerging needs. His positive, professional strategy won the respect of his detractors as well as his supporters.

14. Ability to Compete, Intention to Cooperate

Morton Duetch, in his seminal piece "A Theory of Cooperation and Competition" (1949), states that political conflict cannot be resolved unless two countervailing principles are communicated. If you send solely the message that you want to cooperate, that you will not compete, you will then be violated. You will be run over. Alternatively, if you send the message that you just want to compete with no intention of cooperating, you end up with destructive results, competition to its highest degree. You must send both messages. Whatever you think of President Richard Nixon, he was a master at displaying both notions. He communicated to China that he had the ability to compete, but the intention to cooperate. He was decidedly successful and opened channels of free trade. Jimmy Carter, in all of his benevolent ways, would not have done this—he was too trusting. He communicated only the first of these messages.

15. Win-Win Solutions Win More Than Win-Lose Solutions

It is an old adage by now—"we want to seek win-win solutions." But few parties to a conflict really do anything to promote that. They may use the slogan, but all too often they are really seeking to turn the situation around to make themselves the winner, and correspondingly you the loser. Sometimes the only way to go from win-lose to win-win is to go first through lose-lose—both parties must have something to lose unless they change their behavior.

There's obvious advantage to win-win—not the least of which is that both parties "save face." I remember watching a school district prior to collective bargaining in a process called "meet and confer." District and employee association representatives sat down to attempt to informally arrive at mutually derived labor contract solutions. One of the management strategies was to plot out where the association "negotiators" were on the salary schedule. Once that was done, a new salary schedule was presented that coincidentally created healthy increases to each of the employee representatives, and usually lesser amounts to other association members, particularly inexperienced teachers. A win-win arrangement? Nope!

The process didn't fool the union "negotiators," and they had gone along with a jerry-rigged salary schedule for years. A young high school math teacher figured things out and blew the whistle. The resulting ballyhoo resulted in a turbulent situation. Association leadership and its contract negotiators were replaced. Labor relations with that district were forever negatively changed. To this day, it remains an example of dishonest negotiations by the district in the minds of employees. Lose-lose? You bet. Both the district and the association came out of this with mud on their face. The only place to go from here was up!

It would have been far better to behave in an aboveboard and honest way, searching together for win-win strategies. Both parties took the easy way out and got burned for it. Searching for win-win strategies may take mental toughness and flexible attitudes, but it yields long-term satisfaction and results that stand up to public scrutiny.

16. Count How Many of Your Natural Constituents Are Voters

School people tend to miss some important insights in this strategy. They survey their parents about a bond issue and assume that if parents agree with it then everyone will agree. No! Thirty-nine percent of voters have a school-age child, and that number is dropping, not increasing. That means that 61 percent do not. On top of that, many of the parents aren't registered voters, or if they are, they don't vote. You must keep in mind how many voters really support you. If 51 percent don't support you, go back to the drawing board.

As an elected official, people often said they supported me, but when it came time to stand up and voice their support, they were woefully silent and apathetic. Don't assume support. Gauge it carefully.

17. Celebrate Everything

Celebrating group achievements binds people together. Celebrating small wins along the way helps to keep supporters focused on the goal and lets resistors know that momentum is building in the direction you're heading.

Honoring supporters helps to raise their standing in the organization and gives them added potential influence, which strengthens the whole coalition. Inviting everyone to the party—both supporters and resistors— helps to tear down walls of opposition, build connections among a greater number of people, and spread your power base.

Having fun together makes it harder to stay combative. Even the crankiest resistors find it difficult to frown in the midst of food and laughter.

One year, I was working with a school district that was sorely in need of funds to repair buildings, add classrooms, and expand technology. A steering committee of influential supporters was formed to consider a bond election. A number of the women on the committee reported that, while they backed the idea of a bond for the schools, their husbands staunchly opposed paying any more taxes and were convinced an election would fail. This sowed the seeds of doubt among our supporters. We set out to get an "army of one thousand volunteers" to run the election. We began with a kick-off party and invited our army and their spouses. The high school band played, the PTA provided food and balloons, and speeches honored the community leaders who were fearlessly spearheading this effort.

Our outspoken opponents were amazed by the turnout of volunteers. The huge celebration gave them a sense of the momentum that ultimately carried us to a decisive win. We had a number of strategically placed celebrations along the way to sustain the commitment of volunteers and to continue to build momentum. The fact that our opponents decided to either "hop onto the bandwagon" or stay quiet in the wake of this growing momentum provided the necessary advantage to carry the election.

18. The Theory of Small Wins

I have an experiment that I like to do. I take a carton of buttermilk and choose someone from the audience who loves buttermilk and someone else who dislikes buttermilk. I then ask the buttermilk lover to convince the hater to drink the liquid. He is never successful in getting the hater to drink a whole glass, but he is sometimes partially successful by being able to coax him to take a sip, just a sip (Harvey, 1979). You have to permit gradualism if you're going to be successful.

So, too, with political change. If you propose a change that runs counter to the conventional wisdom or the traditional way of doing things, you encounter resistance. But a way to overcome resistance is to prepare the change on a short-term basis or as an experiment. People may be willing to take a "sip" even if they would never try the whole thing. And we all know of experimental programs that lasted for years and years. So one way to introduce a political change is to try the theory of small wins—a theory of gradualism to overcome resistance. You may be successful by proposing political change in baby steps and by letting each step help you get closer to your goal.

19. Use Conflict Resolution Techniques

In times of conflict, there are a number of techniques that can help you to resolve an unpleasant, and possibly dangerous, political situation:

a. Co-option—assimilating others into a group for the purpose of turning them around.
b. Dialogue—the use of conversation to discuss and resolve an item (Ellinor and Gerard, 1998).
c. Compromise—half-a-loaf strategy.
d. Smoothing—close to avoidance, it is ignoring the heart of the problem and placating the person with whom the conflict exists.
e. Problem solving—use of a systematic approach to resolve the issue, such as those suggested in Harvey, Bearley, and Corkrum (2001).
f. Force—use of command to get compliance.
g. Broken record—saying the same thing over and over and over.
h. Accommodating—cooperating, acquiescing, or giving in.

i. Superordinate goals—the appeal to a higher-order goal than that which the conflict is over.

Table 2.1 displays the conflict strategy that tends to work most effectively with each of the four modes of conflict that may arise in political situations:

1. Heated arguments seem to be the most typical mode for conflict situations, particularly in a political environment. It is imperative to practice self-restraint in these circumstances. It's easy to be drawn into a verbal exchange that you will later regret.

   Outbursts and loud voices can be regarded as bullying—even if you are "in the right" and are being manipulated or badgered. If you are in a public setting, it's best to move the matter into a more private setting. You can include the combatant on a committee (co-option), or you can smooth the situation over by mollifying him with peace-making language and tone. Or you can use a problem-solving technique. You might also use the broken record technique or appeal to a higher value or goal that you both share.

2. In a dispassionate discussion (which is hard to achieved), we can use dialogue or problem solving to resolve the conflict.

3. Where an individual voices a concern, probably stridently, you may wish to include him in a committee to co-opt his assertive opposition. If he isn't a political force to be reckoned with, you may just ask him politely to conclude his remarks and move on to the next speaker, or you can go with the broken record technique. Your other options are to retreat and give in (and sometimes you will have to acknowledge this as the most realistic course of action) or appeal to a superordinate goal.

Table 2.1 Modes of Conflict and Conflict Resolution Techniques

Four Modes of Conflict	a	b	c	d	e	f	g	h	i
1. Heated argument issues	x			x	x		x		x
2. Dispassionate discussion		x			x				
3. Individual voices concern	x					x	x	x	x
4. No resolution is apparent			x			x	x	x	x

4. If no resolution is available to you, you can choose any of the available techniques shown in table 2.1 that seem to have the greatest potential for success in that situation.

SUMMARY OF EXTERNAL STRATEGIES

In summary, there are nineteen external political strategies that the politically intelligent leader will find helpful:

1. Build trust.
2. Create a political vision.
3. You need to meet their needs, or they'll never meet yours.
4. Simplify and clarify your message.
5. Never let 'em see you sweat.
6. Do your homework.
7. Know each decision maker's agenda.
8. Be aware of political blind spots.
9. Coalition building is a long-term and necessary strategy.
10. "Working the community" is usually neither interesting nor fun, but it's necessary.
11. Don't wait to build networks till you need them.
12. Include all sides.
13. Positive responses to perceived dangers win support.
14. Ability to compete, intention to cooperate.
15. Win-win solutions win more than win-lose solutions.
16. Count how many of your natural constituents are voters.
17. Celebrate everything.
18. The theory of small wins.
19. Use conflict resolution techniques.

FINAL THOUGHTS

These nineteen strategies are not meant to be exhaustive, but if you follow them carefully, you'll be able to handle about 90 percent of your political problems. Reality dictates that no matter how good you are, there will always be about 10 percent of your dilemmas that you can't prevent from turning into brouhahas. However, by developing your strategic skills, you will have a much better chance at becoming the politically intelligent leader who has a long career and impressive success in accomplishing the goals your organization needs.

3

Internal Strategies

Internal political strategies are the stuff of good people management skills. If you are managing the internal environment well, you are probably practicing political savvy. However, managing the internal environment can be fraught with controversy, emotional issues, and difficult people. It's not as easy as it sounds. Presented here are eighteen strategies that, if employed skillfully and diligently, will help you become a politically effective leader of people.

THE EIGHTEEN INTERNAL POLITICAL STRATEGIES

1. Build Trust

In chapter 2, we discussed this as an important umbrella strategy for everything else we do in the political arena. Perhaps it applies even more in the internal environment, for these are the people who surround you on a daily basis, year in and year out. Without trust, you can never have the kind of relationship with them that makes it possible for you to do your job effectively.

You will recall that managing mutual trust requires a combination of behaviors on your part:

- demonstrating interdependence,
- speaking and acting consistently,

- honesty in all your dealings with others,
- affability in your interactions, and
- extension of trust to others.

If I show my employees and colleagues that I know I need them and try to meet their needs, and if I act in a consistent way from word to word and from word to deed, and if I act in an honest and forthright fashion, I will begin to build trust with them. In behaving like an affable and sociable person who likes people, others will be more likely to return that behavior. And finally, if I give trust to others, they will be much more likely to trust me.

If I disregard even one of these conditions, then I will compromise trust with my staff and colleagues. Remember, for every ounce of energy it takes to sow seeds of distrust, it takes five ounces to rebuild trust. Neglecting this area is akin to neglecting your garden. If you want to avoid sowing the seeds of dissatisfaction, disappointment, and discontent, it is important to tend your garden of successful teamwork by using healthy doses of the five nutrients listed here. Trust is the prime building block of constructing good teams and enabling good people to become better people.

2. Uncover the Informal Norms ASAP

Norms are "the way we do things around here." These are the guidelines for human behavior in an organization. There are formal, written norms that operate in a few organizations. There are also informal norms—those that we consciously and unconsciously follow but that are not written down anywhere. Especially for the leader who is new to an organization, it is often very difficult to know what these informal norms are (Harvey and Drolet, 2004). And yet it is incumbent upon the politically effective leader to ferret out the informal norms and learn how they weigh things down around here.

When my wife was a new, young teacher, she went into the teachers' room and sat down in a free chair to talk to her fellow teachers. They gave her a funny look and only spoke in one-syllable responses. For the next week, she came into the teachers' room and sat in the same chair. After her first week, one teacher said in a very conspiratorial tone, "That's Peg's chair." She had accidentally sat in the chair "reserved" for Peg. She made an enemy of Peg, and it took months to repair the damage. She had inadvertently violated a silly but important norm. A savvy leader will seek to understand the informal norms and either abide by them or attempt to change them over time.

3. Do Your Homework

This is a corollary of the last internal strategy and of external strategy number 6. You have to ask a number of questions to "know the situation." You need to identify the following:

- What are the key issues internally?
- Who are the individuals or groups that wield power inside the organization?
- Who has a close, if not overt, relationship with whom?
- Who are the independent thinkers?
- Who are the manipulators to beware of?
- What are the hot buttons around here?
- What tends to be persuasive with key opinion makers?

I once knew a community college president who was appointed over the objections of some key staff members. He could solve all the problems that external constituencies posed to him, but dealing with his internal faculty and staff leaders was another case. He used up much of his energy battling with them. He was encouraged by his board to move ahead with needed changes at the college. Doing his homework ahead of time might have helped him to anticipate his staff's actions and reactions. It might possibly have helped him to recognize the hot buttons and sacred cows of that culture. Researching relationships might have helped him to understand the power structure he was dealing with. Perhaps he could have avoided some of the manipulators who tried to take advantage of his lack of knowledge of the organization to sway him to take actions favorable to them. Getting some help in doing his homework from an objective coach could have helped him see his way through dealing with all the factions of this very complex situation.

4. Dig the Well Before You're Thirsty

This is the corollary to external strategy number 11. You can't wait until you have a problem to begin to establish your power base in the organization. That's too late.

Take a sincere interest in people at all levels of the organization. Learn about them and what's important to them. Look for common ground with a wide variety of individuals and groups. Develop allies who have shared interests. These are people that will keep you informed about what's going on in the organization. You cannot operate in a vacuum. It's not good for the organization if their leader is flying blind. They will let you know about political blind spots. They are the ones who will carry your message and tell your story to others. And they are more likely to stand with you when you are under attack. Connect early and often with people to build your networks and coalitions so that they are there for you when the need arises.

The CEO of a university foundation was very skilled at this strategy. His ultimate goal was to raise money for the university, but way before he ever asked people for donations, he would invite them to "friend-raising" events. These were social occasions where there was an opportunity for alumni and VIPs in the community to gather together to enjoy delicious refreshments and have some entertainment provided by the university drama or music departments. Later, some of these people might be invited to serve on advisory committees or on the foundation board of directors. Still later, they would be asked to donate personally and to contact others with whom they had connections to ask for their donations. This CEO knew how to "dig the well before he was thirsty."

5. Link Agendas

In *Getting Past No*, William Ury makes the point that "you usually can't satisfy *your* interests unless you also satisfy the other side's" (1993, p. 18). Political effectiveness means that you have to work skillfully with people who have different values, priorities, interests, and goals, without giving up what the organization needs to sustain success. "Agenda linking" has been called the "cornerstone of all strategies for working the human system" (De Luca, 1999, p. 95). When you link your goal to someone else's, you gain support for your proposal.

Finding these commonalities requires that you ask questions and pay attention to the answers. To discover a person's real interests, look beyond her stated positions. Listen to what she says in other settings. What does the grapevine add to understanding the interests behind her positions? It's not always an accurate source of information, but it can provide you more clues to check out. How does she behave when this topic is raised in meetings? Is she positive and interested, or bored and disgruntled? Even when a person does not articulate a position, you can learn a lot about their real concerns by being observant and asking questions. Knowing what someone's real values and priorities are helps you to develop proposals that will let you advance your agenda by helping her to advance hers.

Crucial to finding those win-win proposal elements is examining your own interests and alternatives. Distinguish your wishes from your bottom-line needs. Brainstorm options that meet your essential criteria.

For example, employees of a large county office wanted a raise. The county office was facing a budget shortfall and had an offer of zero on the table. Skyrocketing health insurance costs were contributing to the budget crisis. Although the stated union position was a salary increase plus continuing their benefit package, a problem-solving dialogue produced a resolution that linked both agendas. The union agreed to increasing deductibles and co-pay, as well as to changing providers. This allowed the county office to recover enough insurance costs to give the employees a better raise and keep their coverage. The negotiators found a way to link agendas to produce a successful outcome.

6. MBWA—Management by Walking Around

In the crush of paperwork and perpetual problems, some leaders have become desk and phone bound—and now many have become e-mail junkies! They find it harder and harder to "come up for air," which leads to isolation and lack of information.

Get out of your office and walk around! Stop in. Visit your people. Visit those in other departments. Ask about their families, their weekends. Ask what's going on and how thing are going. Listen!

You pick up a lot of information when you stick your head in an office and talk to people at all levels in the organization. And being seen makes you more real, more approachable if problems come up that you should know about.

One department head literally avoided walking through his department by entering through a side door. He said he didn't want to talk to people because he was an introvert and being with people drained his energy. His staff interpreted his actions as having no interest in them, no respect for their contributions, and no concern for their problems. When his staff became aware of a problem in his department, they didn't bother to go to him with it. They let it escalate to the point where it became an explosive issue.

The next leader made it a point to walk through and greet people each morning, interacting with them on a human level and showing concern for the problems they were having on the job. His availability and approachability made his staff feel comfortable in letting him know of pending issues before a crisis started brewing.

7. Be Open to Their Ideas

Listen to all their ideas, not just the ones you want to hear, because when you honestly listen, you show respect for others. You respect their thoughts and opinions and honor them as persons. You've seen elected officials who, with crossed arms, just pretend to listen. Everyone can see that they have their minds made up before they give you the time to speak. They disrespect you. What do people do when they feel disrespected? They speak out; they backbite; they sabotage; in short, they get even.

Just as you are open to your own "superior ideas," you must be open to your peers' and subordinates' thoughts and opinions. You might find some nuggets contained in their thoughts, but even if you don't, you must show consideration and respect. This is just good management, but it is also good internal politics.

8. Empower Others

You empower those around you

- when you give them important work to do,
- when you grant them discretion to do their work,
- when you give them the resources to do their work,
- when you give them praise and recognition,
- when you make them feel that their survival is in their own hands,
- when you enhance and build task skills,
- when you encourage them to work in teams, and
- when you welcome surprise. (Harvey and Drolet, 2004)

When you do all or most of these things, you empower your subordinates. But why do you bother? Because the more power you send away, the more power you'll get back. If you empower people, they will think you're astute and perceptive and a superior leader. They will do "anything" for you. Conversely, if you don't empower people, they won't give you the time of day.

I remember this with great pain. I had a college president who focused only on himself. He took credit for everything. He looked over everyone's shoulders. He constantly emphasized that without him, the institution would fall apart. He controlled every decision. He even demanded that the employees throw him a "surprise" birthday party, yearly. They hated him, and he had *no* political power to get things done. Whatever he wanted, the opposite would get done. He tried to keep the power to himself, and hence he had no power. After six years, he died in his office.

9. Make Use of the Chit System

"Scratch my back; I'll scratch yours." That, in a nutshell, is how the chit system works. The story I told you earlier about the utility manager and the eventual energy crisis is a good example of this. She did so much for various cities—she had earned so many chits—that when it came time to help her with legislation on the energy crisis, we gladly accommodated. She traded chits.

The same can be done internally. When I was dean, I went out of my way to fund various departmental programs and to advocate for these programs to upper management. When I got into trouble with that upper management, the department chairmen came to my rescue and argued that without me they couldn't do their job. They saved me. But if I hadn't built up a lot of chits, the department chairmen would have stood on the sidelines and let me wallow in my problems. Chits had been successfully traded.

The key in trading chits is that the leader goes first, without expectation of return. This revisits the concept of making a lot of deposits so that you'll have a large balance when you need to make a withdrawal.

10. Expand the Pie with "Out of the Box" Thinking

During times when resources are insufficient to maintain current services, the natural temptation is immediately to look for cuts. This usually means loss of valued people and programs—in other words, giving everyone a smaller piece of the resource pie, and some may get none.

However, a better approach might be to look for ways to expand resources first with entrepreneurial or intrapreneurial activity. Clients and staff members appreciate this effort. It helps them to truly understand the nature of the problems, and it helps them to see you less as a bureaucrat and more as an empathic, creative leader. It gains support and can even reduce political backlash if the extra resources cannot be produced.

In one district, we had a serious budget crunch looming on the horizon. We were faced with major cuts and layoffs, and we were looking for a creative solution. We had one school that was built on an unusually large site facing a major thoroughfare. We decided to divide the site, using the acreage facing the major street in an entrepreneurial way. We leased the front third of the site to a developer to build a senior citizen facility, which produced an ongoing revenue stream for several decades and then returned the site and the facility to the district. The back two-thirds was ample for the school, which fortunately had another entrance from a neighborhood street.

We were able to solve our revenue shortfall with "out of the box" thinking.

11. Many Messengers—Same Message—Bigger Impact

People are naturally change resistant, unless they invent the change. If you are the only one advancing an idea, it's doubly hard to get support. Involving others in creating the change helps to build a cadre of supporters.

Leaders frequently serve as the spokesperson for a new idea for three reasons:

1. They enjoy the credit and attention for new creative ideas.
2. They feel they understand it best and can present it with the most clarity and persuasiveness.
3. They yield to pressure from supporters who want them to be the spokesperson. Subordinates believe that it will be easier to get support from resistors if they know the boss approves, and it takes the heat off them.

Big Mistake! People tend to believe their peers about the worth of an idea much more than they believe their boss. They usually feel that their peers understand the complications, the extra workload, and the downsides of any change. They feel that the boss is too far removed from implementation to truly understand what it will take to make this change happen. They often believe that the boss "has to support the change" whether she truly feels it will work or not. And most of all, they don't like changes "rammed down their throat" by the leader.

For all of these reasons, it makes so much more sense for the leader to resist being the sole spokesperson for any proposed change. You are more likely to get support for a new idea if you step into the background and let your supporters step forward to make proposals.

It's also important to share the credit and the limelight with the staff members who have been instrumental in creating the new ideas. They deserve the recognition, and this is the way to build more leaders.

For example, if you use a committee of stakeholders to develop a facilities plan, let them present it to their respective groups and to the governing board. If there are resistors, this takes courage. Those who are willing to step up to the plate need to be encouraged, rewarded, and protected by their leader. You need to think this through ahead of time, have honest discussions with them about how to proceed, and consider the timing and process you use to make the presentation. Involving people the staff respects, along with those who usually complain, can create a more receptive environment. Using this strategy in combination with other strategies on this list will increase the receptivity quotient.

12. Be Aware of Internal Political Blind Spots

We discussed political blind spots under external strategies. They can also exist internally in the organization. For example, as a new leader in the organization, you may decide on a more efficient way of setting up the office and direct people to move their desks to new locations. Sounds like a simple change, right?

What you may not know is that there are several locations in the office that are set aside as a result of years of maneuvering and negotiating by the people who have been around the longest. These little pieces of "real estate" are the most coveted locations and are "owned" by the most senior staff regardless of what makes the most sense for office operations. This decision—which seems like a prudent business move—can cause an uprising that can become very ugly for the new leader.

It's important to seek out the political blind spots before you make decisions affecting others. Talk to people, ask questions, observe, and bounce ideas on trusted supporters or colleagues to uncover those blind spots before acting. And then ask yourself if this is an idea that needs to be taken forward at this time.

13. Where Snipers Dwell, Plan Meticulously

Of course nothing improves your chances for success like good planning! Planning backward, with clear vision of your outcome to guide your actions, helps you to anticipate potential obstacles, needed resources, and consequences connected with various alternatives. Planning enhances effectiveness and efficiency and smoothes the way for implementation in a timely manner.

However, in a toxic environment, planning is no longer a nicety—it's a necessity! Toxic situations usually harbor snipers—people inside or outside your organization that lie in wait, taking shots from cover at those advancing changes or advocating positions that the snipers don't support. In this situation, imagining how your words or behaviors can be taken out of context or misrepresented will help you to be proactive in structuring your messages or determining your actions.

Years ago, I was appointed the chief negotiator of union contracts in a district where there had been a history of adversarial relations with the district administration. A new school board and a new administration had been put into place before I arrived. What I failed to realize was that the union had supported the campaigns of four of the newly elected board members, and the lines of communication between them were very good. I soon learned that the union would caucus and call the board members during a negotiating session if they didn't like the district's proposal. Although I had received my bargaining parameters from the school board, board members were calling me away from the table to question my tactics as they were described by the union representatives.

To counteract what I viewed as sniper attacks, I went over everything with the board ahead of time, explaining my strategies, and I even asked them to send one of their own members to the table with me to observe the dynamics firsthand. I was confident that my strategies were fair, ethical, and aboveboard. Therefore, it was in my best interest to have a board observer report directly to her colleagues what was happening. That ended the attacks and built my credibility with the board. It also built my credibility with the union negotiators because they could see for themselves that I was implementing the board's direction.

14. Go Slow to Go Fast

When we are excited about a new idea or under stress to move forward with a needed change, we can very easily get ahead of ourselves. We may be tempted to move fast toward final decisions and implementation because our "close associates" support it too. This is the time when we need to put the brakes on and let the others catch up.

Moving too fast usually means that not all of the stakeholders are "up to speed" on your new idea. Even if they are generally supportive or laissez-faire in allowing management to make the calls, if they get confused, don't understand the plan, or can't comprehend how it will affect them, you run the risk of major resistance—later if not now.

Moving too fast also may mean that you haven't analyzed potential blind spots or unanticipated consequences.

Take the time to bring everyone into the loop. Getting involved with them in dialogue, answering their questions, giving them examples of how it would work, showing them other places where it's been successful, and asking their advice and guidance in designing some of the implementation aspects—all will go a long way toward getting all stakeholders together. Baby steps—that's the way to bring people along at a comfortable pace.

In the public sector, policy decisions are under the watchful eye of the media, stakeholder representatives, and special interest groups. Elected officials may have been informed early on in the process and may be generally supportive. But that can change in a nanosecond if the voters start writing, phoning, and turning up at board or council meetings.

Sometimes constituents can become enraged after a decision is announced if they have not had the opportunity to have their "say" beforehand. The public tends to see their elected representatives as not representing their best interests if the representatives do not listen respectfully to the public's input before making major decisions that affect them. This rift in their relationship can also cause a rift in the relationship between you and your governing board or council.

In most cases, it pays to "go slow to go fast." If you take the time to do it right beforehand—to build support for your idea among all stakeholders first—you are more likely to be able to move expeditiously once you have the green light to go.

15. Benevolent Environments Yield Risk-Taking and Creativity

It's obvious! Where the climate of the organization is good, where there is trust built up, where people act in astute political ways, there is much risk-taking behavior; there is much seeking of feedback, negative and positive; and there is much creativity and attempts at innovating.

On the other hand, where the climate is toxic, where backbiting and rumormongering are routine, where a lot of "political games" occur, everyone in the organization "covers his or her own backside" and is self-protective. This is an environment where risk-taking and creativity shut down.

It is so simple to understand but so hard to do. We pollute the political environment a piece at a time—to a point that it is so polluted that it is indelibly toxic. Pollution can happen fast, so care must be taken to constantly cultivate that benevolent environment that promotes risk-taking, innovation, and creativity.

This is done by rewarding those who are willing to constructively criticize new proposals or ideas for change. This is done by eliminating the cult of "yes-men" from the organization. It's done when the boss is able to laugh at herself and nurture the problem finders as well as the problem solvers. It's done in an environment where people find joy in the workplace, are treated with respect and dignity, and are encouraged to take reasonable risks without fear of penalty for failure.

These are the kinds of environments that are open to change and improvement—the cornerstones of successful, sustainable organizations.

16. Knowing Who Trusts Whom

When you are trying to enlist support for your ideas, you already know that presenting a strong, rational case does not always get it done. You have to be able to persuade people that your idea is worth the risk of putting themselves on the line for an unknown outcome.

Human behavior tells us that we are more likely to get on board if someone we trust says that they are ready to get on board too. The skill comes in finding out who trusts whom.

Networking and MBWA can help you identify people who respect and trust each other. What frequently helps us garner support is to determine whose approval you need, and then to find the person that he or she trusts and respects. If you can persuade that person to join your efforts, you may have found the one who can help you convince needed others to support your proposal.

Looking at the basic political unit of all time—the family—we can find many common examples of this principle. If a young teenage son wants to go on a church ski weekend and Mom is opposed to nonfamily weekend trips, he may ask Dad's help in persuading Mom that the trip is a good idea. The young skier is tapping into the fact that Mom trusts Dad's judgment, and his support can be very helpful in influencing her decision.

In our earlier example of the chief negotiator whose school board was being influenced by union leaders, taking a board member to the table helped to persuade the board that negotiations were being handled properly. They were willing to listen to one of their own board members who was an eyewitness to bargaining discussions because they trusted her.

17. Float the Idea

Whenever you are pursuing a new idea, it's unwise to take it into a room full of people who know nothing about it. It's far better to wait until you have a majority who at least has learned about it from you or one of your trusted emissaries. In smaller groups, they need to have had a chance to ask questions, discuss the proposal, hear the potential downsides that might be pointed out later, give their input, and indicate whether they are willing to talk about it further in a larger meeting.

It's not necessary, and in some cases it may be unwise, to ask how people will vote ahead of time, but it is necessary that they have plenty of time to assure themselves that this is a viable idea worthy of further discussion. If you can incorporate any of their input into the project, that makes it all the more attractive.

What we have observed in many situations is that people who know nothing about an idea, or who are confused by the way it's presented, are very unlikely to support it on the spot. Giving them a heads up as to what it's all about and how it can affect them is more likely to at least make them want to explore it further.

Additionally, floating the idea can help you to continue to improve the proposal and the presentation, since you will know what's clear and what's not, what's persuasive and what's not.

18. Use the Accordion Process to Increase Involvement

When input from many people (more than thirty) is desired or needed in developing a product or making a decision, you can

1. include all people in the decision-making team or
2. exclude them from the team and notify them of the decision or
3. make a series of incremental decisions with a small team and then go out to the wider constituency to seek input and reaction while the decision is still in the formative stage.

Including a great many people directly on the decision-making team is usually unwieldy and inefficient, as well as ineffective in designing quality solutions or changes. Excluding them altogether destroys trust and support for the outcome.

It is the third alternative that we suggest as most effective. By going from the small committee to the larger constituency and taking their input back to the small committee, you involve the whole group. In this way, you get both input and ownership. The idea may or may not be improved, but politically everyone feels consulted. And buy-in means follow-through on the change and implementation with less resistance.

SUMMARY OF INTERNAL STRATEGIES

There are eighteen strategies that can help the politically intelligent leader deal effectively with internal political situations:

1. Build trust.
2. Uncover the informal norms ASAP.
3. Do your homework.
4. Dig the well before you're thirsty.
5. Link agendas.
6. MBWA—management by walking around.
7. Be open to their ideas.
8. Empower others.
9. Make use of the chit system.
10. Expand the pie with "out of the box" thinking.
11. Many messengers—same message—bigger impact.
12. Be aware of internal political blind spots.
13. Where snipers dwell, plan meticulously.
14. Go slow to go fast.
15. Benevolent environments yield risk-taking and creativity.
16. Knowing who trusts whom.
17. Float the idea.
18. Use the accordion process to increase involvement.

FINAL THOUGHTS

While we have divided the strategies into two categories—external and internal—it is possible to use some of these strategies outside the category in which we describe them. They are divided here to give you an idea of which strategies offer significant advantages in dealing with outside forces and which offer vital benefits in working through internal situations. However, a strategy described in the external section can often offer a great deal of promise with an in-house situation, and vice versa.

As you begin to practice using these strategies, it's important to remember this guidance. These eighteen strategies can be used separately, but combining two or three together increases their power exponentially. These strategies come with a moral imperative to use them for good purpose in helping you to accomplish noble goals in an ethical manner.

II

ANALYZING POLITICAL STYLES

4

Understanding Your Own Political Style

Personal competence is knowing yourself and doing the most you can
with what you have.

Travis Bradberry and Jean Greaves,
The Emotional Intelligence Quick Book

POLITICAL STYLE—WHAT IS IT?

Who among us has not been burned by someone skilled at intrigue and
manipulation? We may have been run over by a "political truck" and
never even seen it coming. Not everyone uses their political skills with
ethics and integrity. Adding to the perils of encountering "sharks" in the
organizational sea, public sector organizations like education are gener-
ously populated with idealistic, trusting individuals whose job training did
not include organizational politics.

The result, often, is that they feel inadequate to compete in the political
arena. They try to avoid political situations and political people. Unfortu-
nately, they can run but they can't hide from politics, and the politically
intelligent will have the best chance of surviving and thriving!

Those who shun political situations tend to believe that they are apolit-
ical and therefore don't have a "political style." But everyone has a political style—even when they are contemptuous of politics. Self-awareness
is the first step toward the competence that will help you deal more effectively in this arena.

In his book *Political Savvy*, Joel De Luca (1999) points out that developing your political competence requires that you understand yourself and your political style. Your political style is composed of a set of values, preferences, and priorities that are reflected in your behaviors and attitudes. They color your sense and understanding of people and situations. They influence your reactions, your initiatives, and your comfort level.

While one might have a "default style"—the one that tends to be the style they use in most situations, or that they revert to in stressful situations—it's not unusual to move into the behaviors of other political styles when the situation calls for it. It is also possible to change your political style if it's not working for you. This requires a commitment to learning through study, observation, analysis of behaviors and consequences, coaching, action planning, and follow-through.

All too frequently, we go through life unaware of our own political style and its impact on our organization, as well as of how much it influences our success in our career and personal relationships. In this chapter, you will learn what makes up a political style and what characteristics typify nine different styles. You will also have the opportunity to take an instrument called the Inventory of Political Styles (IPS) to help you determine your own default style, as well as your backup styles in various situations. This instrument is presented here, and it is recommended that you take this assessment now before you read on. When you finish, score it and then move to the pages explaining the various styles. See Appendix: Inventory of Political Styles.

Understanding Your Political Style

The Inventory of Political Styles is designed to give you insights about your own political style. Knowing your default style, as well as your backup styles, helps you to understand more about yourself and the way in which you tend to operate in politically stressful situations.

Improving our political acumen also means understanding the political styles of others. A keen awareness of the values, priorities, preferences, behaviors, and attitudes of others helps us to predict how they will react to our proposals, what strategies they will use to assist or sabotage our ideas, and how best to win their support. We will deal more with this in chapter 5.

ELEMENTS OF POLITICAL STYLE

De Luca (1999) developed nine political styles based on action orientation and "attitude toward politics." His work inspired our somewhat different analysis of political styles in the public sector. While we agree with De Luca's suggestion that action orientation—or, as we see it, degree of initiative—is a component of style, we believe that a much stronger determinant of style for educational and public sector leaders is their goal allegiance, that is, their commitment toward advancing goals—their own or their organization's.

Goal Allegiance

In education and other public sector roles, people tend to operate on a continuum from an exclusive focus on goals associated with self-interests to an exclusive focus on goals associated with organizational interests. For example, an individual who doesn't show up at an important awards ceremony for his students because someone gave him tickets to the playoffs is more focused on a goal reflecting self-interest. Firemen who are willing to sacrifice their lives to protect their community are motivated by goals that have a strong organizational interest. Most people move back and forth somewhere along the continuum depending on the circumstances. Your political style is associated with where on the continuum you tend to focus most consistently.

Your goal allegiance is determined by looking at how you react, not only when it's easy, but when the situation makes it hard to choose between goals that further your own interests and those that further your organization's interests.

Basis for Goals		
Self-Interests	Blended Interests	Organizational Interests

Figure 4.1   Goal Allegiance Continuum

Political Initiative

Once you have a goal in mind, whether it's for your self-interest or your organization's interest, the question is, what do you do about it? Again, people tend to function on a continuum somewhere between passive and assertive. Those who are reluctant to take risks, to get involved in complex situations, or to engage with others tend to be less likely to take action. They are guardians of the status quo, bound by inertia. They find themselves closer to the passive point on the continuum. People with passive styles are sometimes impressed with what the assertive styles can accomplish and with the courage they demonstrate. On the other hand, they often feel that the assertive types can cause trouble for the organization, can put others in jeopardy, and can be foolhardy in their lack of caution.

At the other end of the continuum are those who are eager to take the plunge, anxious to make things happen, and disdainful of the indecisive. Their passion for action must be tempered by patience and reason. They are the bold drivers of change and innovation, for better or worse. Their style will be characterized by assertiveness, and they are willing to put themselves on the line with their ideas and opinions. While the assertive styles tend to be willing to take center stage to advance a cause, there are some who prefer to stay in the background and exert their force through others. Those with assertive styles are sometimes impressed with the way passive people can stay out of the "line of fire," and they appreciate it when the more passive members provide the support needed in accomplishing the goal, but they typically tend to have greater respect for the assertive styles, even when they are on opposite sides.

While individuals may move back and forth along the continuum depending on the circumstances, they may feel more comfortable closer to one end or the other, and their styles may be shaped in part by their proclivity toward assertiveness or passivity—especially in times of stress.

Goal Focused Political Styles

Political style is formed at the intersection of these two continuums. It is a combination of your goal allegiance—self or organization—and the degree of initiative you tend to commit in accomplishing that goal—passive support or assertive action.

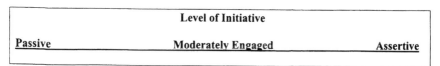

Figure 4.2   Political Initiative Continuum

Goals of self-interest or organizational interest trigger the degree of action that an individual will take in any given situation. They also influence the "default style" that is characteristic of that person.

Additionally, while there is a strong tendency for one political style to be the "default style," our model recognizes that situations can propel an individual into other styles, which they may adopt consciously or unconsciously, temporarily or indefinitely. Often, individuals will have a style that they tend to use most of the time, but they will also have a strong backup style that may look somewhat different. It's important for organizational leaders to recognize their preferred style, their backup styles, and also the styles that they are least likely to use. In this way, they can be more deliberate about the political choices they make, rather than operating on autopilot now and regretting the consequences later.

THE NINE POLITICAL STYLES

In contrast with De Luca's grid (1999), our matrix reflects styles that are a blend of the degree of initiative and goal allegiance each style has. Leaders can have a strong commitment either to self-interests or organizational interests but lack the initiative to take the action necessary to advance those interests. However, the goals that drive them will determine the direction of their political action and may even influence how assertive or passive they will be in a given situation.

The nine political styles displayed in table 4.1 represent intersecting preferences for using one's initiative and goal allegiance. It combines passivity with three loci on the goal allegiance continuum—self-interests, organizational interests, and a midpoint between the two poles, which we call blended interests. It also combines assertiveness with each of these three places on the continuum. And finally, it combines the midpoint of initiative, which we call engaged, with the same three places on the goal allegiance continuum. This produces the nine styles displayed in the matrix and which are described in more depth below. Each style has some advantages and disadvantages. How the style is used determines its value to the organization, to the stakeholders, and to the individual.

Table 4.1   Political Styles Matrix

GOAL: INITIATIVE:	Self- Interests	Blended Interests	Organizational Interests
Assertive	Challenger	Arranger	Strategist
Engaged	Planner	Balancer	Developer
Passive	Analyst	Adaptor	Supporter

The Analyst

Typically passive in their approach, *analysts* are more dedicated toward self-interest. They take a self-protective posture in the face of proposed change. They are concerned about changes that will disturb what they are good at and comfortable doing. They are slow to take any risks, since they have little trust for others in the organization and have seen leaders come and go. They often believe that many past changes have had little success and no longer have a place in the organization. They are wary of the swinging pendulum of changes that have cost time, effort, and money over the years. This causes them to analyze proposals carefully, looking for possible problems and hidden costs. They do not want to be guinea pigs or be out in front of potential changes. They need evidence of success before they can even consider moving toward a change. Their need for evidence, proof, and demonstrations slows down any organizational changes.

On the other hand, their caution can have the advantage of making others plan more thoroughly, anticipate consequences more carefully, and consider all alternatives before embarking on an innovative course that can cost the organization time, resources, and political fallout.

The Adaptor

Another passive political style is the *adaptor*, who is midway between self-interest and organizational goals. Adaptors are generally supportive of the direction of the organization. They value their job, and keeping the organization strong ensures their own stability and security. They understand the organization's culture and are willing to learn new ways to support the organization's direction. Supervisors can usually count on their support for changes that will help the organization, as long as it doesn't put them at risk. Even when they can see a problem with a proposal, adaptors rarely point it out or raise questions, not wanting to appear resistant.

Their cooperative nature makes them valued staff members—someone who can be counted on to support the team and good naturedly adapt to new ways. However, the adaptor's unwillingness to overtly question new directions or make waves is a disadvantage to leaders who need candid input from all sources. Too much unquestioning support may result in leaders moving too fast and not considering all consequences and alternatives.

The Supporter

An enthusiastic devotee of the organization's vision and goals, the *supporter* is a positive representative to the public. As enthusiastic as supporters are, they are still risk aversive and are therefore passive in any political activity that would impact the organization or jeopardize their career. Their positive nature helps to keep optimism alive in the organization. They avoid discord and rather than take sides will quietly support both parties.

Because they avoid conflict, they will not be helpful in resolving important issues that arise. Their tendency to quietly support both sides causes others to lose trust and confidence in the validity of their comments. Their optimism can sometimes mask critical flaws that should be addressed in any new plan.

The supporters' strength is that they are committed to the best interests of the organization. They inject harmony in team settings and provide encouragement for the pioneers of new ideas. When an idea finally gets off the ground, the supporters' value to the team is that their enthusiasm can be contagious and can help to build momentum.

The Planner

Exercising moderate initiative in political activity, the *planner* is focused more on personal goals rather than the organization's interests. Prior to taking any real action, planners assess risk to their own security. Planners are very careful and vigilant in the way they go about their political activity. They outline options and seek as much information as possible about each of them.

The planners' value to the organization lies in their ability to collect data, lay out alternatives, and analyze outcomes. Their skill in generating data and trends provides valuable insights to leaders about implementation details. Their focus on details makes them ideally suited to edit documents and keep track of agreements, minutes, applications, and other documentation. They generally understand the law, regulations, and policy and can help to ensure that the organization stays on the right side of all of them. They will develop timelines and benchmarks for projects and are willing to send reminders to others when due dates are nearing.

Planners will engage in political activity as long as it's fairly safe to do so. This limits their effectiveness when they are in disagreement with those higher on the organizational ladder. They may hold back ideas and information if they feel the personal risk is too great, even when the organization is going through difficult times. Their effectiveness can be enhanced by ensuring nontoxic environments, where people are made to feel safe in sharing ideas or disagreeing with a direction.

The Balancer

Midway between passive and active, and also between self and organizational commitment, the *balancers* are at the fulcrum of the political spectrum. Their ability to see all sides of the issues helps them to encourage fairness and consideration of all parties and concerns. They have a blended orientation of self and organization. They see that their success is very much tied up with the organization's success, and therefore they do what they can to support and promote organizational goals and directions. They understand the importance of networking, and they promote the culture of the organization through storytelling. They feel that the organization's best interests are served when people are happy and satisfied in their work. They like to see all parties attempting to "meet each other halfway." Balancers empathize with those who are attempting to improve the organization but are careful about taking risks before they know more about the potential outcome.

The balancers' value to the organization rests in understanding the culture and how people will respond to proposed change. They look for solutions that will bring people together. They communicate with a lot of people in the organization and therefore understand how different aspects of proposals will be accepted by others. They also may know what the real interests are that various parties have, even when their position may be stated differently. However, their preoccupation with morale and norms can sometimes impede progress and cause the organization to give up some of the more important aspects of a change plan.

The Developer

Committed to the organization's goals and priorities, the *developer* is willing to engage in moderate levels of political activity to ensure needed change. The developer recognizes the importance of helping other stakeholders grow in their skills and insights to enhance their contributions to the organization. The developer also coaches and supports them in their desire to advance their personal careers and status if they demonstrate loyalty to the vision of the organization.

Developers help the organization by empowering others with knowledge and skills. They are perceived by many to be valuable to the organization and are respected by those in power. They assist leaders in planning, anticipating issues and consequences, and selecting strategies that will enhance chances of successful adoption of proposals. Although they are willing to engage in some political activity to serve the organization's goals, they prefer to stay behind the scenes. They are less likely to undertake any action that could put their job or their reputation or their connections to power brokers at risk. The developers' reluctance to step up to using greater initiative in political action keeps them from being as powerful a force as they might otherwise be.

The Challenger

Confident in their own vision, ideas, and goals, *challengers* "need to lead." They form unusual strategies not necessarily understood or expected by others. Comfortable with command positions, they are quick to give direction and make decisions. This may result in cutting others out of the process, which may lead to lack of support and resentment. They are politically active and aggressive in pursuing their goals. They are extremely task oriented and are very inventive in developing the means to their goals.

While they are able to turn on the charm selectively, diplomacy is not their natural mode. They have little respect for passive members of the organization and really don't see their role as nurturing others. They enjoy being the "movers and shakers" and frequently say, "I'm not here to win a popularity contest." However, they often believe they are more popular than they are. Their feedback mechanism may not be very well developed, since they can be oblivious to the reactions of others. Their "thick skin" allows them to move ahead without worrying what other people may think of them or their course of action.

The challengers' value to the organization is their efficiency in getting the job done and their willingness to take a leadership role in high-risk situations, which might be avoided by less confident people. Also, in some stagnant, resistant, or failing organizations, a challenger may be useful in providing the strain necessary to change direction.

However, the challengers' lack of consideration for the contributions and concerns of others can lead to short-term achievement and long-term dissatisfaction. They tend to accrue opponents who are willing to wait as long as necessary to "get even" when a challenger has stepped on toes once too often.

The Arranger

Midway on the continuum between self and organizational dedication, the *arranger* is very assertive in using initiative to pursue goals. Arrangers help to make things happen. They are well connected in a variety of arenas and have skills in diplomacy that are useful in forging alliances and negotiating deals. They are generally liked and respected by colleagues, followers, and supervisors. They can tap into many sources for information necessary to produce effective change. They recruit supporters for change proposals, and they work on the logistics to facilitate implementation. They love the "art of the deal" and are very creative in generating interesting solutions to complex problems.

The arrangers' value to the organization is their skill in building coalitions and orchestrating presentations to decision makers. They also are invaluable in planning strategically to bring their ideas to fruition. They have the courage to take risks to pursue their goals. They are very task oriented, and their contributions could be strengthened with better listening skills and collaborative processes.

The Strategist

Highly active in pursuing initiatives that advance the vision of the organization, the *strategist* is a futurist and a coalition builder. Strategists have the courage to take reasonable risks in support of the organization's major goals. They are willing to put themselves on the line to accomplish an organizational need. They are imbued with the values of the organization and model its beliefs. They empower others and encourage their creative energy. They are "door openers" rather than "door closers" to ideas offered by others.

The strategists' value to the organization is visionary leadership with practical implementation of creative ideas. Strategists involve others in collaboration to design and market proposals because they believe that involvement produces new and better ideas and promotes buy-in among those who will implement change. They are skilled in building networks of support for the organization in general and in specific change efforts. They use a variety of strategies to gain approval of new platforms and commitment to the organizational vision.

Strategists are excellent tacticians, capable of devising plans to gather and maintain support. However, strategists can devote so much time and energy to their political activities that they suffer burnout. Idealism can result in disappointment when change is blocked or slow to succeed.

Having a strong team is crucial to a strategist to avoid these pitfalls and maintain a strong level of energy and mental outlook.

INTERPRETING YOUR POLITICAL STYLE

As we said earlier, individuals may have one style that they tend to use when things are going their way, and possibly another, completely different style when they are under fire or in uncertain times. To help you interpret your own style, we have asked you to calculate your three highest and your three lowest scores. This will tell you the styles that you tend to use the most, and the ones that you are least likely to use.

The styles that you use the most are the ones that feel the most comfortable to you—either because you have the most practice with those behaviors, because you've had the most successful outcomes with them, or because you have not ventured out to try other styles, even when what you're using isn't working all that well.

And the styles you are least likely to use are the ones that feel most uncomfortable, unfamiliar, or unattainable. It's rarely a style that you've discarded because it's not working for you, because we find that people seldom are aware of alternative styles or even how their own behavior may be contributing to political failures. Using the Inventory of Political Styles will give you an opportunity to become more reflective about your action or inaction, and the goals that are steering your exploits. Examining your styles and how they are working for you will help you to be more deliberate in your choices.

It is very unlikely that someone would be Johnny One-Note when it comes to political style. Almost everyone has backup styles that they use depending on the situation. As you consider your scores, look at the descriptions of each of the styles that received your highest scores. Highlight or underline the words that you feel apply to you. Put a box around the words that don't apply to you.

Reflect on the situations where those styles emerge. When do you tend to use those styles? What's happening in your environment? Is that style working in that environment? If it is, why is it working? If it isn't, why not?

To help you think through your political style scores and how to interpret them, consider the scenario below.

> Ed is in a middle management role. He's working in a large, toxic organization with snipers everywhere, and with an unpredictable CEO. He may feel the need to function in survival mode — unlikely to take risks or move too quickly to engage in much change or innovation. He likes his job and depends on the income. If the CEO wants a new direction, Ed will get on board with it, even if he sees some holes in the idea, because he feels that to do otherwise would threaten his security. However, he will be slow to implement, in case things go wrong. In meetings where there is conflict or controversy, he "keeps his head down" and his "flak jacket" on. Ed is an adaptor in this situation.
>
> On the other hand, within his own department, Ed may function very differently. He has cultivated a positive, supportive culture among his staff members. He is committed to the people who work for him. He appreciates their hard work, and in turn they trust him to help them be successful. They enjoy the work they do together. He coaches and mentors them. He is skillful at working behind the scenes to find resources they need to be efficient and effective. He helps them to advance in their careers. In this environment, Ed becomes a developer.
>
> In yet another environment, Ed may have yet a third alternative style. He may enjoy an active leadership role in a service club, with many supportive colleagues who are working to support cancer research, a cause near and dear to him, since he lost his father to this disease. He has a reputation in this club for successful fund-raisers, and so he uses his initiative to plan even bigger and better fund-raising events. He may use his connections with other members who work in city hall to negotiate special venues for a big event, police assistance with security, and special permits for vendors. He may persuade the club to back the event with a larger percentage of their budget because he is confident of the public interest and support. In this situation, he is willing to take greater risks and put himself on the line because of the supportive context and the organizational goals to which he's committed. Ed is an arranger in this environment.

Adaptor, developer, and arranger — three very different styles. Ed's highest scores and the styles which are most comfortable for him vary according to his present situation.

In looking again at his scores on the IPS, Ed may find that his lowest score is the challenger. He would probably not be as comfortable in command roles, where there is little collaboration with others in solving problems and planning for the future. While there are situations where he would put himself on the line for his organization, he does not enjoy high-risk maneuvers. He is willing to make changes, but he goes about it in a more methodical way with consideration for the feelings of others. He would not be comfortable if his actions alienated others or caused a rift in their relationships, and he might sacrifice a needed change in order to preserve relationships.

Another low score might be the strategist. He is willing to take some risks but does not see himself as a terribly courageous person who is willing to "tell it like it is." He has made use of the connections he has through some of his organizations, but he does not really enjoy networking and coalition building. Ed has a family and likes to take them camping and to sporting events. He may not have the willingness to commit "whatever it takes" in time and energy to an organizational cause.

Possibly a third low score would be the analyst. His organizational goals pull him away from the passivity and self-interest that characterize the analyst. While there are situations that cause him to take a more self-protective posture, his concern for those he works with balances it out. He is often fearful of change in this toxic environment, but he is disdainful of foot-dragging for its own sake. Sometimes Ed doesn't have the patience to look at every little piece of documentation or to insist on evidence of success before agreeing to implement something he's asked to do. There have been times where he's had defects in new products because of this lack of attention to detail.

Understanding what helps you and what can hurt you in the style preferences you have, as well as what you lose from styles that you may tend to avoid, will help you to develop the insights you need as you make deliberate choices in honing the styles you use in the future.

FINAL THOUGHTS

Every individual has a default style and one or two backup styles. Which style they use depends on the situation, their comfort level with the style, and the consequences of using the default or backup styles.

Every organization has individuals of all styles—and that's a good thing. Organizations need planners and adaptors and developers and strategists. And they also need analysts, supporters, balancers, and arrangers. On occasion, challengers can play a helpful role.

The key is to raise your political styles to a new level of consciousness so that you can function deliberately with the behaviors that will serve the best interests of you and your organization. Then you must develop your skills in utilizing that style to its greatest advantage. The following chapters will help you with that skill building.

5

Working Effectively with Other Political Styles

No man is an island, entire of itself.

John Donne, Meditation XVII

Donne's familiar words remind us that people do not function in isolation one from the other, but are interconnected and interdependent in their lives and in their organizations.

To function effectively in this system of connectedness, we must not only be aware of the strengths and deficits of our own political style, we must also understand how to work with others who have a whole range of styles. In chapter 4, we discussed the nine political styles and analyzed our most and least used styles. In chapters 2 and 3, we examined various strategies that are available to us in improving our political efficacy with organizations and situations.

In this chapter, we'll bring styles and strategies together as we discuss how to select strategies that tend to resonate with people of particular styles that you'll encounter.

We'll explore each of the nine political styles from a different perspective. Instead of analyzing our personal political styles, we now turn our attention to those whom we encounter in our work. Knowing their political styles will help you to understand what they need, want, and disdain in their interactions with you.

DECIPHERING THE STYLES OF OTHERS

How do you know what political style another person has? Can you give them the Inventory of Political Styles to assess them? Of course not! So you have to fall back on your experience in working with them.

- What is their goal orientation?
- What is their political initiative level?
- What key words do they use to give away their style?
- How do they behave in politically charged situations?

These are the key questions you must ask yourself to gauge their political styles. You proceed cautiously, always aware of new data that may alter your perceptions.

STYLES AND STRATEGIES

Once you know an individual's style, you can turn to the following list of strategies and determine which ones will have the greatest probability for helping you to enlist their support for your proposals. Not all of these strategies will work 100 percent of the time with all individuals. As you now know, not everyone is a pure example of just one style. Situations and other players also influence the way in which people respond to our overtures. And of course, our expertise in using these strategies is a great determiner of effectiveness. As in any other skill, practice promotes proficiency. We are generalizing here to help you get an understanding of how to apply these ideas in your organizational setting.

If one were to exploit these strategies for unethical purposes or personal gain, that person would be guilty of the kind of manipulation that calls politics into disrepute. However, employing these strategies in an ethical, aboveboard way enables you to use politics as a powerful and positive tool to deliver your organization's vision and to achieve noble goals.

Let's turn now to a view of each of the nine political styles as they might exist in others. The following material focuses your attention on the types of behaviors you are likely to observe so that you might be able to diagnose their styles. We will also discuss what strategies have the greatest potential for gaining their support. A summary box for each style pulls it all together in short form for easy review and reference. And a real-life example for each style shows you how to apply your learning.

WORKING WITH ANALYSTS

Since analysts lean toward security, you will probably observe risk avoidance in their behavior. They respond well to concrete data where you can show them proof that your idea is working elsewhere. They are unlikely to support proposed changes that are brand new and have never been tried, simply on the strength of a promise of a good return on their investment. While others may be inspired by exciting ideas, logic, and projections, the analyst is more likely to say, "Show me the goods, the outcomes, the results."

Analysts like to see it in writing. They want to analyze all the alternatives, the anticipated and unanticipated consequences, and what it's going to cost them in time, resources, and political fallout.

Since analysts are security conscious, they want to know what the decision maker's agenda is. Before going too far out on a limb, they will likely want to know what kind of support has been proffered from those higher up in the organization's food chain. Even if you take them to see a new program in operation at another site; they will not be the ones to take the first leap. More probable for them is to take baby steps in the direction of the change, with lots of opportunity to stop and make midcourse corrections if necessary. With the analyst, you "go slow to go fast." Taking the time to answer their questions and satisfy their concerns up front will increase the likelihood of their support and speed up implementation in the long run.

Since making their own decisions has some risk attached to it, they are most likely the people who will say, "Just tell me what you want me to do." That way, if it hits the fan, they will not be the ones to get blamed.

The analyst understands "chits." He's a realist. If he owes you a favor, he will grasp the unspoken assumption that he needs to reciprocate from time to time if he is to expect more favors in the future.

The analyst is more likely to get on board if she hears from many sources that this is a good idea and it's going forward, so we need to support it—especially if she trusts the messenger.

If there is conflict over a change, the analyst can be co-opted by involving him in some of the planning and problem solving. If given a direct command, he will respond with support—at least on the surface.

For example, if you want to introduce new accounting software to Andy Analyst, you might want to build trust by talking honestly with him about the reasons you are seeking a change in the software. You could ask him what he needs to feel comfortable with the new software acquisition. You might involve him in developing the criteria for selecting new software.

Here are some other strategies that might help Andy come to a supportive posture with regard to this change: Use concrete examples in looking at all the alternatives, weighing them against the criteria, and assessing the positive and negative consequences of each. Invite him to join a group that will visit at least one—and preferably more—site where the software is currently in use to assess its effectiveness. Let Andy talk to

---

WORKING WITH ANALYSTS

Look for these attributes to determine if you are working with the *analyst*:

- Self-interests
- Passive
- Risk aversive
- Needs proof
- Very cautious
- Likes alternatives
- Weighs consequences
- Security conscious

Strategies that work with the *analyst*:

- Build trust
- Use concrete examples
- Approval of power structure
- Go slow to go fast
- Chits
- Many messengers
- Co-option
- Command
- Broken record
- Meet their needs
- Link agendas

people who have actually implemented the change in question so that he can assure himself that he will be safe if he supports it in your organization. Get the support of the CEO and let Andy know that the boss is all for it. Design an implementation plan that will provide for careful training and let him take baby steps in the transition expectations.

Andy may continue to come up with reasons not to change the software. Going broken record with him may help to convince him that the need for new software is not going away. Occasionally, Andy may just not want to cooperate on a necessary change, and he may resist past the point where you have no choice but to invoke a command to implement the change.

WORKING WITH ADAPTORS

Adaptors do not lean toward self-interests as much as analysts, and they are not as inclined toward organizational interests as supporters. However, they have the same level of passivity as both. Adaptors care about their organization's health and stability, in part because it affects their own security.

They will adapt to changes proposed by the organization's power structure. They are open to getting as much training as necessary to be sure they can perform adequately with anything new. Because they worry that questioning proposals or changes will make others feel that they are unsupportive, they need a very safe environment and a great deal of encouragement to tap their honest insights and concerns.

For example, in working with Alice Adaptor on a staffing change that will put her in a new position, it will be important for her to know that the provost wants it to go forward. Praising her work and recognizing her contributions to the organization will help to put her at ease. Hearing about the benefits and simplicity of implementation from colleagues she trusts will tend to alleviate her concerns.

Alice needs to understand how it will affect her personally and exactly how much training will be provided. If her workday will be lengthened during the transition, she'll want to know about overtime pay or comp time. Although she'll want the change to be successful for the organization, she will be reluctant to point out any potential problems she might see for fear of being perceived as uncooperative by her boss. In order to draw her out and get her advice on making the most effective change, you need to reassure her, positively reinforce her for her contri-

---

WORKING WITH ADAPTORS

Look for these attributes to determine if you are working with *adaptors*:

- Blended interests—self and organization
- Passive
- Risk aversive
- Security conscious
- Need to feel competent
- Reluctant to point out problems

Strategies that work with *adaptors*:

- Build trust
- Go slow to go fast
- Agenda linking
- Praise and recognition
- Many messengers
- Command
- Broken record
- Meet their needs
- Simple messages
- Do your homework
- Use norms
- MBWA
- Be open to their ideas
- Create a benevolent environment
- Where snipers dwell, plan meticulously
- Know who trusts whom
- Conflict strategy of smoothing

---

butions, and make sure you don't react sharply even to possible criticisms from her.

It's far better to use a smoothing strategy with Alice if there are disagreements in how to implement the change, rather than involve her in conflict. However, she will respond to a command if ultimately one needs to be given.

WORKING WITH SUPPORTERS

Supporters are basically positive, optimistic team members who enjoy harmonious relationships. They do not respond well to conflict, heavy-handed tactics, or negative behavior. They look for the silver lining and are willing to extend trust to their bosses and others. They are not likely to hurt others, and they don't want to be hurt themselves. They avoid risky situations and are unlikely to be in the group that is willing to "stand up and be counted" if there is any controversy.

Supporters respond well to testimonials from people they trust and to success stories related to proposed changes. They are eager to please the organization's leaders, and therefore their boss's support of a change will be important to the supporter. They like simple, clear messages that show how a change will advance the overarching goals they support.

WORKING WITH SUPPORTERS

Look for these attributes to determine if you are working with *supporters*:

- Dedicated to the organization
- Passive
- Risk aversive
- Positive and optimistic
- Avoids conflict
- Harmonious
- Cooperative

Strategies that work with *supporters*:

- Build trust
- Testimonials from trusted sources
- Approval of power structure
- Go slow to go fast
- Agenda linking
- Superordinate goal
- Expand the pie
- Many messengers
- Problem solving
- Meet their needs
- Simple messages
- Do your homework
- Celebrate everything
- Use norms
- MBWA
- Benevolent environment

Because they are unlikely to risk failure, they prefer to move slowly into a change, and they want to be sure that problem-solving mechanisms are part of any transition process. They enjoy celebrations and are inspired by vision, access to their leaders, and an environment that is open and encouraging.

For example, in working with Sally Supporter on establishing a new reading intervention program for low achievers at your high school, you will be most successful if you practice management by walking around (MBWA) and have developed a relationship with her earlier. Encouraging her to speak openly about her classroom successes and her concerns helps to build a trusting relationship. This is necessary if she is to embrace this change, and it will help you to determine what might be on her agenda. In this way, you can look for ways to work together to accomplish mutual goals.

Her agenda might be to stay at this school, where many of her friends work and where she is well liked by the parents. Since the district is considering moving staff if the test scores do not rise, you can help her to achieve her goal if she can help you to improve test scores by developing this new program.

Doing your homework to discover unwritten norms that may influence the procedure that Sally and her colleagues would want to use in developing this new reading program is essential.

WORKING WITH PLANNERS

Planners are very careful about their own security. However, they are not willing to be completely passive about engaging in political activity if it's to advance their own personal goals. Their cautious nature leads them to ask a lot of questions and seek the kind of information that will help them to develop a set of plans to accomplish their goals. Making yourself available for Q-and-A sessions will help the planner feel more comfortable with a proposed change.

Planners pay attention to details and respect those who do their homework and can describe how the details will be handled. Handouts at meetings will help them take notes and will alleviate stress. Planners like to know that leaders have gathered data to support their proposals. They want to see it for themselves and look for trends and loopholes. They are well organized and have a good command of policy, rules, and regulations.

Planners are not likely to put the organization ahead of their own objectives or convenience. For this reason, they can slow down change initiatives and can appear to be uncooperative. They understand that knowledge is power and may not always be willing to share the abundant information they have gathered, especially if there's a risk of offending those in power.

Because they are risk aversive, they are looking for signs that the leader is confident with the proposal. If there are any signs of worry or nervousness, they are likely to oppose the plan.

WORKING WITH PLANNERS

Look for these attributes to determine if you are working with *planners*:

- Engages in moderate level of political activity
- Self-interests are the priority
- Risk aversive
- Well organized
- Lots of questions
- Slow to change
- Not likely to speak up in public or in meetings
- Holds back information
- Uses data to develop careful plans

Strategies that work with *planners*:

- Win-win
- Agenda linking
- Chits
- Many messengers
- Command
- Broken record
- Meet needs
- Simple messages
- Never let 'em see you sweat
- Do your homework
- Respond positively to perceived danger
- Count your votes
- Use norms
- Dig the well early
- Create a benevolent environment
- Where snipers dwell, plan meticulously

For example, in working with Patrick Planner to negotiate a new labor contract, it will help if you have created a benevolent environment where he is comfortable expressing his views and opinions to you firsthand. This will help you to understand his agenda so that you can craft a win-win solution. Inviting him to sit on the budget committee so that he can have direct access to all of the data on revenues and expenditures and can get all of his questions answered will help him to understand your needs and interests. Prepare handouts with all of the budget data from the last three years to show trends in income and spending. Use simple, clear statements to explain the fiscal picture, rather than financial jargon.

Do your homework to learn more about the politics of his environment. If he is getting pressure from his union members to increase the salary to exceed the mean of comparison districts, look for creative ways to try to meet his needs without jeopardizing your own. Looking at the mean of each cell on the salary schedule may show that some already exceed the mean, and boosting those that don't—rather than applying the same across-the-board increase to all—might be within the dollar parameters you have from the board.

Going broken record on the district's needs and proposals will help to impress Patrick that other tactics will not change the district position. If he threatens the board with a strike, it's important not to let him see any expression of panic or anxiety. This is the time to be confident and courageous.

WORKING WITH BALANCERS

Balancers are a blend of organizational and self-interest and are moderately engaged in political activity to support the goals they consider to be important. Balancers don't like conflict and will do what they can to avoid it. They respond well to those who are interested in preserving employee morale by looking for solutions to problems.

They are well networked in the organization, and people tend to share their true feelings and details of their situation with balancers. They tend to know the backstory of many people in the organization, which makes them valuable in identifying blind spots, as well as potential incentives and interests of staff and community.

Balancers tend to think that most problems can be solved by meeting each other halfway. Giving up half of what your goal is does not generally provide the best solution for either side, and therefore leaders need to work with balancers to generate other solutions. Helping them to look behind positions to identify interests will assist in that.

Balancers understand the culture, they bond with colleagues, and they tend to stay in their positions for long periods of time. They prefer to use strategies of problem solving, smoothing, and dialogue to resolve conflict. They will have more respect for you if they perceive that you too are part of networks and coalitions that can help you to accomplish your goals.

Using the accordion process as a tool to get many others involved in considering new proposals will appeal to the balancer, who prefers to have the support of peers before moving ahead.

For example, if you are attempting to develop a logistical plan for a major modernization project for your facility, which will result in staff being rotated in and out of their classrooms over the course of a year, here are some strategies that may well appeal to Bert Balancer. After doing your homework to uncover any blind spots and relationships that could help or hinder the project, establish a committee that includes Bert and his peers—some of whom are cooperative and understand the need, and some of whom are unwilling to be inconvenienced. Meet with each person ahead of time to learn more about their interests and needs. Develop norms together that will guide the committee in working together and coming to consensus.

Use clear, simple statements to identify the problem and get agreement on what the problem is. Establish criteria for selecting the best solution. In an open, benevolent environment, dialogue and a problem-solving model can help you to generate solutions that meet the criteria.

When you have a solution that seems to meet the criteria, the accordion process of getting reactions from those affected will produce more insights. It's important to be open to feedback that comes in so that you can craft a final solution that has buy-in from most of those affected. Bert will probably respond well to these efforts and will help to sell the final solution to his peers.

WORKING WITH BALANCERS

Look for these attributes to determine if you are working with *balancers*:

- Goals will be a blend of organizational and self-interests
- Moderate initiative
- Avoids conflict
- Avoids risk
- Seeks stable morale
- Well networked
- Trusted by others
- Longevity in position
- Meet each other halfway

Strategies that work with *balancers*:

- Build trust
- Go slow to go fast
- Win-win
- Agenda linking
- Superordinate goal
- Expand the pie
- Include all sides
- Accordion process
- Conflict strategies
- Problem solving
- Political vision
- Meet their needs
- Simplify your message
- Do your homework
- Know each decision maker's agenda
- Be aware of political blind spots
- Coalition building
- Working the community
- Build networks
- Respond positively to danger
- Count your votes
- Use norms effectively
- MBWA
- Be open to ideas
- Empower others
- Create a benevolent environment
- Know who trusts whom
- Float the idea
- Accordion process

WORKING WITH DEVELOPERS

Developers are true believers in the organization's goals and are willing to become moderately engaged in advancing them. They have a great deal of information and insight about how to produce the needed results, but developers prefer to stay in the background and help others perform in the limelight. Although this makes them valued members of the team, they cannot be counted on to be the spokesperson for change.

Developers value trust and trustworthy people. Therefore, in working with them, it's important to dig the well early in building a trusting relationship. Once trust is broken, it's very difficult to get them to trust again. They respect those who are courageous and fair-minded and who show grace under pressure.

They prefer to invest time and resources in preplanning to make sure that the project rolls smoothly once it's under way and to forecast any potential barriers to success. They see the value of including all sides in problem solving and would be wary of any committees that seem one sided. They respond well to norms and believe that norms provide fair and equitable treatment of committee members and ideas.

Developers appreciate those who look for ways to "expand the pie" rather than dismantling valued programs. They do not respect people who try to take short cuts with process or jump too soon to expedient conclusions. They admire those who do their homework, are creative in linking agendas, and have a political vision.

Developers also make networking a priority. They believe that it's important to learn about the agendas of decision makers at all levels, and they see this as a way to build relationships that can help the organization.

For example, if you wanted to create a proposal for expanded parkland that would be supported by both city council and school board members, Donna Developer on the school district staff could be a great asset. Having spent the last year working closely with her, you have built the trust necessary to float this idea and get her advice. Referring to a conversation with your city manager, whom Donna has known for many years and both respects and trusts, share with her the reasons you believe the parkland is essential. Mentioning the superordinate goal of service to families and youth, which is a priority in both city and district visions, can help persuade her of the importance of this idea.

WORKING WITH DEVELOPERS

Look for these attributes to determine if you are working with *developers*:

- Dedicated to organizational goals
- Moderately engaged in political activity
- Shies away from the limelight
- Prefers stability but will take limited risks for the organization
- Trust is a high priority
- Looks for fairness and equity
- Likes to preplan to avoid mistakes
- Likes to help others plan and prepare
- Respects those who do their homework
- Networks effectively to establish power base for the organization

Strategies that work with *developers*:

- Build trust
- Go slow to go fast
- Win-win
- Agenda linking
- Superordinate goal
- Expand the pie
- Include all sides
- Accordion process
- Problem solving
- Create a political vision
- Meet their needs
- Simplify and clarify message
- Do your homework
- Know each decision maker's agenda
- Be aware of political blind spots
- Coalition building
- Working the community
- Build networks
- Respond positively to perceived danger
- Celebrate everything
- Use norms effectively
- Dig the well before you're thirsty
- MBWA
- Be open to their ideas
- Empower others
- Create a benevolent environment
- Know who trusts whom
- Float the idea
- Where snipers dwell, plan meticulously

Knowing that resources are already allocated to existing programs, you might ask her who could be helpful in brainstorming ways to "expand the pie." Let her know that you want to spend sufficient time preplanning this proposal to ensure that you have something that will ultimately be supported by the board and council. Get her input on potential committee members who would be inclined to support or oppose this project.

Show Donna that you have done your homework by reviewing those people in the networks you have that would be likely allies in putting together a coalition to support the project. When it comes time to present the idea, ask for Donna's advice on how to do it, but don't expect her to stand up in a public meeting and speak out in favor of it. She might be able to suggest someone else from the district's staff and help them prepare their speech.

And, once the park is ready to open, don't forget to plan a huge celebration and invite all the key players who put it together!

WORKING WITH CHALLENGERS

Working with challengers can be one of your most exigent and intimidating political encounters. Challengers are self-oriented and assertive. They are confident in their own views and believe in their own ability to lead, but they frequently do not respect those with less assertive political styles. They are typically decisive and scorn those who take too much time to "get things moving." They like the limelight and getting credit for their accomplishments. They are task oriented, and they value efficiency rather than focusing on a process that takes more time but makes people feel that their input is valued.

While they are willing risk takers, they also want to be aligned with the top decision makers. Therefore they respond well to knowing what the president, chancellor, superintendent, city manager, or electeds want.

They also respect someone who demonstrates that they have the ability to compete but the intention to cooperate. You can never let challengers see you sweat when the "heat is on." They will lose respect for you, and it may bring out their aggressive side if they think you are an easy mark. While the challenger would seldom choose to include all sides in making a decision, it can be a very effective strategy to use when you need to keep the challenger "under control" or slow him down if he is steamrolling along.

Always do your homework when dealing with the challenger. You can be more effective if you know his agenda. It may aid you in developing a proposal in which he can win one of his goals by promoting your goal. MBWA helps you to keep abreast of what the challenger might be doing behind the scenes. It will also help you to gather information about your potential political blind spots. When dealing with a challenger, the more information you have, the better you will be able to handle political issues.

Dig the well early as you build your networks and coalitions. This broadens your power base and lets the challenger know he is dealing with more than one individual if he "takes you on." Networks can help you head off any moves the challenger may be planning to resist or discredit your proposal.

Challengers may choose unusual means to reach their goals and can often surprise you at moments that can make you look unprepared, incompetent, or incoherent. It's important to plan meticulously in working with a challenger, especially if his network or coalition includes snipers.

Having a political vision to keep you clear on your values and priorities will serve you well in dealing with challengers, who can pull you off course if you don't have a compass.

For example, in working with Charlie Challenger to try to build a new student resource center for the university campus, it would be helpful to let him know that the university board of trustees has identified this project as their number-one priority.

If his ideas are to divert funding for this project to one of his own, it may help to activate a committee of staff and community leaders and bring Charlie out into the open. Including members of your coalition on this committee will help to increase the number of messengers who can express the importance of this project to students and to the university. Using the accordion approach to involve even more stakeholders can increase your power by increasing stakeholder buy-in.

If Charlie tries to wear you down with alternative proposals, the broken record approach may be a good tool to use. However, it's important to remember that the challenger may have some good and valuable ideas, so don't turn a deaf ear to him. Listening to Charlie's suggestions may give you some insight into possible places to link agendas and develop a win-win solution, where you both are able to achieve your goals by helping

WORKING WITH CHALLENGERS

Look for these attributes to determine if you are working with *challengers*:

- Self-interests are priority
- Assertive
- Self-confident in vision, values, ideas
- Comfortable with command role
- Task oriented
- Creative with means to goals
- Diplomacy not valued
- Not nurturers
- Movers and shakers
- Efficiency is prized
- Do not respect passivity
- Willing to take risks
- Want the credit for achievement

Strategies that work with *challengers*:

- Include all sides
- Win-win
- Agenda linking
- Chits
- Many messengers
- Ability to compete; intention to cooperate
- Broken record
- Never let 'em see you sweat
- Do your homework
- Know each decision maker's agenda
- Be aware of political blind spots
- Coalition building
- Plan meticulously where snipers dwell
- Working the community
- Build networks
- Respond positively to danger
- Dig the well early
- MBWA
- Be open to their ideas
- Know who trusts whom
- Use the accordion approach
- Count your votes

each other. Paying attention to his criticisms of your proposal will help you to improve your own plans and be ready to articulate your rationale for your final proposal.

Plan meticulously when you are dealing with Charlie. A challenger will take advantage of weaknesses, loopholes, and oversights. You are likely to have blind spots, and working with trusted associates to identify them can save you from making damaging mistakes in your strategy.

It's also important for you to know who trusts whom in your organization, since they can be useful in influencing the final decision makers—in this case, the university president and the board of trustees. Gaining the support of the opinion makers can be a real asset in determining the final outcome. Involving them on your committee or using informal networking are a couple of strategies that may be useful here. Count your votes, and don't bring the matter to a formal judgment until you are relatively confident in the support you have among the decision makers.

WORKING WITH ARRANGERS

Arrangers are very assertive in pursuing their goals, which are a blend of both organizational priorities and their own interests. These diplomats are generally charming and articulate in explaining ideas and expressing feelings. They like to deal with others who are skilled at finding common agendas and crafting deals that break stalemates.

Arrangers understand the importance of building their power base by connecting with many people. They are part of numerous networks, which facilitates coalition building when they need it. arrangers respect others who have broad power bases and who have the intention to cooperate but the ability to compete.

They are willing to take risks to advance their goals and are strategic in combining resources. They can be more task oriented than people oriented. At times, their efficiency gets in the way of their effectiveness.

Do your homework when dealing with arrangers. Be sure you know where the potential blind spots are. Keep in touch with what the decision maker's agenda is, and be guided by your own political vision. When you are dealing with assertive, politically active styles, you must be prepared for surprises and ready to implement new strategies.

Working the community can be very valuable in dealing with arrangers and challengers. Not only do you develop strong networks, but a wide range of people come to know you firsthand for your true ideals and values. It also helps to identify who trusts whom in the power structure of the community.

Arrangers respect those who can be creative about "expanding the pie." They enjoy problem solving and dialogue to resolve conflicts and will also resort to smoothing. They like to deal with people who are willing to meet their needs, and they will reciprocate if they can. Because they are open to the ideas of others, they can be vulnerable to snipers. While they are willing to take some risks, they do not like to get involved in ugly situations, preferring to arrange things in advance so it doesn't come to that kind of conflict.

For example, Arthur Arranger is the diplomatic college dean and is an ambassador between warring departments on the university campus. He is well received by faculty in both departments and is skilled at putting together solutions for difficult problems. The two departments tend to be in conflict over resources.

In working with Arthur to secure support and funding for a new program, you might float an idea for it first. Knowing that Arthur has a trusting relationship with the department chair who supports your idea may mean that you schedule a three-way meeting to discuss the idea.

Showing how this new program could better address the superordinate goal of serving students more effectively would appeal to the dean. However, Arthur would want to see that you have done your homework, analyzing alternatives, consequences, costs, supporters, and opponents. He would also want to know where the blind spots are in securing faculty support from both departments under him. If you can show him that you have ideas as to how to expand the pie, Arthur will be more receptive, since finances are a zero-sum game in this university.

Arthur would want you to include all sides in refining this proposal. He would hope to avoid any escalation of hostilities between the groups and would be very open to any proposal that would begin to unite them. Arthur will have his own thoughts on how to adapt the program, so it's important that you remain open to his ideas. Ask his advice on how to move forward.

WORKING WITH ARRANGERS

Look for these attributes to determine if you are working with *arrangers*:

- Blended organizational and self-interests
- Assertively pursues goals
- Diplomatic
- Skilled in crafting deals
- Many networks
- Coalition builder
- Risk taker
- Strategic
- Task oriented

Strategies that work with *arrangers*:

- Build trust
- Win-win
- Agenda linking
- Superordinate goal
- Expand the pie
- Include all sides
- Accordion process
- Conflict strategies
- Problem solving
- Political vision
- Meet their needs
- Do your homework
- Know decision makers' agenda
- Be aware of political blind spots
- Coalition building
- Working the community
- Build networks
- Ability to compete, intent to cooperate
- Respond positively to danger
- Count your votes
- Celebrate everything
- Use norms effectively
- Dig the well early
- MBWA
- Be open to their ideas
- Empower others
- Know who trusts whom
- Float the idea
- Accordion process
- Where snipers dwell, plan meticulously

WORKING WITH STRATEGISTS

If you are working with strategists, you have the advantage of knowing that they tend to "walk the talk" of the organizational values, and therefore you are more likely to know what motivates them and what is likely to turn them off.

They are open to new ideas and are usually approachable by those who have creative proposals if they trust you. Therefore, it's very important to build a trusting relationship with them early on. Candor, cordiality, and consistency help to build that trust over time so that you have it when you need it.

Strategists value ideas from all sides and therefore tend to place more confidence in proposals where there is a process in place to seek that input. They respect someone who is assertive enough to take the risk of initiating dialogue and problem solving with others around the concerns that may arise over a proposal they have put forward. They admire those who model grace and courage when under fire.

Strategists like ideas that are presented in a clear, crisp, simple manner. They often have creative ideas of their own to contribute and tactical solutions for breaking through barriers to implementation, so they want to be heard. Unless their ideas detract from your original intent, incorporating their thoughts will help you to achieve their buy-in.

Because of their skill in political tactics and networking, strategists can be powerful allies or awesome adversaries. They will tend to respect those who have the ability to compete but the intention to cooperate. Their networks and coalitions are widespread and influential. Therefore, it is imperative not to take their good nature for granted. You must do extensive homework and learn who is in the circle of trust that can make a difference in getting your proposal approved. Find ways to link agendas, and you'll enhance your chances of success.

For example, in working with Stephanie Strategist to get some help with a proposal to establish a new in-house "birth to age ten" child care program for employees, doing your homework can produce important information. For example, Stephanie has no children and therefore would not need this service personally.

Through MBWA, you discover that Stephanie is looking for more resources for a new program she is trying to initiate. However, you also

WORKING WITH STRATEGISTS

Look for these attributes to determine if you are working with *strategists*:

- Organizationally oriented
- Assertive
- Risk taker
- Models the organizational values
- Empowers others
- Open to new ideas
- Visionary
- Creative
- Networks
- Tactician

Strategies that work with *strategists*:

- Build trust
- Include all sides
- Win-win
- Agenda linking
- Superordinate goal
- Expand the pie
- Accordion process
- Ability to compete, intention to cooperate
- Dialogue
- Problem solving
- Political vision
- Simple, clear message
- Do your homework
- Know decision makers' agenda
- Be aware of political blind spots
- Coalition building
- Working the community
- Build networks
- Respond positively to danger
- Count your votes
- Celebrate everything
- Uncover informal norms
- Dig the well early
- Link agendas
- MBWA
- Be open to their ideas
- Empower others
- Benevolent environment
- Know who trusts whom
- Float the idea
- Use the accordion process

learn that her assistant has missed a lot of work because of child care issues, and this has caused project delays and no small amount of frustration among coworkers. You now have uncovered a reason for her to oppose your project—the drain on resources she needs for her own goals. And you have discovered a reason for her to support your project—fewer potential absences by her assistant.

While Stephanie is not the decision maker, she is very influential in the organization. Floating the idea with her first will give you the advantage of getting her reactions firsthand before going to decision makers.

Since "people first" is one of the organization's values, you might develop a clear and simple proposal to present to Stephanie, showing how it can benefit the employees, the children, the department heads, and the organization. Focusing on the superordinate goal of people first and the family values of the organization will appeal to Stephanie's commitment to the organizational vision. Showing her how this program can reduce employee absenteeism has the added dimension of meeting one of her goals and helping the organization as well—a win-win solution!

Since funding will be one of her major concerns, you might suggest getting a few people from your network together to brainstorm ways to "expand the pie." Sharing ideas like grant writing, child care fees, and partnering with other organizations like community youth-serving agencies may spark her creative side. Be open to her ideas. Also, suggesting a committee that would involve those affected, as well as some of the department heads, might be a way to generate more solutions to potential issues.

FINAL THOUGHTS

Working with people of other political styles can be a tricky business. The complexities can be overwhelming unless you take the time to understand the people and the situation. Using the political tools provided here will help you to individualize your approach. The ability to customize your strategies gives you a greater potential of success in influencing the level of support you receive from others. This valuable asset will enhance your personal effectiveness and your chances of successful leadership in your organization.

III

STAYING ON AN ETHICAL COURSE IN POLITICALLY CHARGED SITUATIONS

6

The Politically Ethical Leader

> Ethical decision making requires more than a belief in the importance of ethics. It also requires ethical sensitivity to implications of choices, the ability to evaluate complex, ambiguous and incomplete facts, and the skill to implement ethical decisions effectively.
>
> Michael Josephson, *Making Ethical Decisions*

Ethical dilemmas with political consequences! These are the dreaded quagmires that often drive good people away from leadership roles. Determining right from wrong is not always as simple as it used to be in Sunday school. The nuances of situations can sometimes make it difficult to select the right action from among many alternatives. And the threat of dire political consequences—even when you make the choice that's right for the organization—can add anguish to the stew of frustration and depression that can be cooked up in these situations.

This chapter is designed to help you confront your ethical dilemmas and give you some ways to reflect on the link between ethics and politics.

DEFINING ETHICS

Ethics is defined here as a set of principles determining that which is right or wrong in human conduct. These principles, says Stephen Covey, are "not invented by us or by society; they are the laws of the universe that pertain to human relationships and human organizations" (1991, p. 18). He places honesty, integrity, trust, fairness, equity, and justice in this category. Principles help to shed light on our options and provide a compass to guide us through a maze of choices.

As individuals, we form our own opinions about what's right and wrong. We are influenced by religion, family values, friends, personal experiences, education, organizations, and professional codes of conduct, to name a few. The values that we develop in the process of living may or may not be shared by others, and unless they are aligned with universal principles, they may not always be helpful in clarifying our ethical options as we deal with organizational dilemmas.

Conflicting values exist not only among people but also within an individual, and this adds to the complexity and confusion when sorting out a moral dilemma. There are many examples of this.

Most Americans would agree that preservation of life is morally right, desirable, and admirable. Ordinary people have risked their own lives to save a person, whom they don't even know, from a burning building. Complete strangers have volunteered to donate a kidney to someone who would die without an imminent transplant. However, when the question changes to preservation of life in an unborn fetus, a wide chasm has emerged between those who are "pro-life" and those who are "pro-choice," and there are many who consider themselves to be both.

In the first half of the 20th century, discrimination laws still prevailed in the South. Obeying the law is generally considered ethically right. But when the law kept black children out of white schools and black women on the back of the bus, that value conflicted with the value of social justice—and the civil disobedience movement erupted across this nation.

Stealing would be considered wrong, but if a homeless child stole some bread to help his starving sibling stay alive, how would that be regarded? Employees who have waited three years for a fair raise may view the actions of a CEO as morally reprehensible when she rejects their demands and puts a recent windfall of money into building maintenance. However, newly discovered mold and dry rot in the walls and ceilings may be a higher priority for the CEO who is concerned about client and employee safety. Which should take precedence?

Even when you are clear about your principles, making ethical decisions is not as easy as we would like it to be. It's complicated by situational nuances, details, and perceptions. It's complicated by conflicting values. And it's complicated by the political environment of your organization.

A MODEL FOR MAKING ETHICAL DECISIONS IN TODAY'S POLITICALLY TURBULENT ENVIRONMENT

Whenever there is enormous change, coupled with high expectations and competition for resources, a tide of emotions will often sweep the organization, leaving loss, frustration, grief, and anger in its wake. Moral dilemmas arise, and power and politics enter.

While we can cognitively accept that disturbances in changing organizations are "normal," leaders are often thrown off balance as they try to deal with the turbulence, disorder, and even violence that may emerge. The challenge for the leader is to keep his emotions in check, stay on an ethical course, and make politically viable decisions that move the organization forward toward its vision.

The Organizational Politics and Ethics Model (figure 6.1) shows the leader's path to ethical, politically viable decisions that advance the organization's goals. The leader operates within a sphere of influence. He functions in a context that includes organizational vision and values, a variety of constituencies, and diverse communication channels. The context is rife with conflicts of all kinds. There are overt and covert norms guiding the behavior of those inside and outside the organization. Some of these norms are commonly held. Some are not.

Working in this context, the leader must work through murky moral and political dilemmas. She is guided in that work by superordinate goals — goals that are overarching, bigger than the day-to-day agendas that leaders typically need to advance. Superordinate goals are those that are the beacons of light in an organization, such as placing "children first" as a priority in decision making at an elementary school. These are the goals that most of the stakeholders in an organization recognize as preeminent.

To work effectively with individuals and groups, the leader needs to use prudent judgment in combining what he knows about ethical principles and managing ethical conflicts, along with political strategies. Combining his knowledge and skills in these crucial areas will help resolve moral and political dilemmas. Together, he and his stakeholders will be able to develop

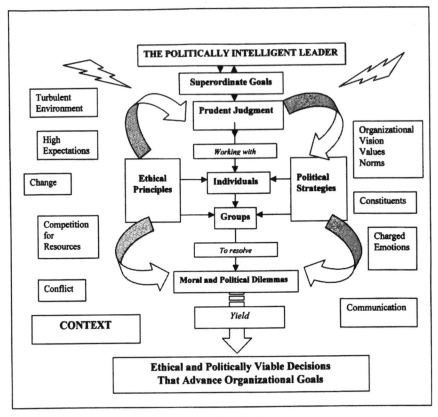

Figure 6.1   Organizational Politics and Ethics Model

sound ethical decisions that have the political support necessary to advance organizational goals.

IT'S ALL ABOUT MAKING CHOICES

As you have seen from earlier examples, choices don't come labeled "right one" and "wrong one." Often you're choosing between desirable and less desirable alternatives. Sometimes, an alternative might even be legal, but is it the right thing to do? Today's civil rights violations may have been considered "legal" throughout much of our history, but were they ethically right?

While goals are important for any organization, choosing an unethical means to accomplish an ethical goal is a lure that traps many well-intentioned leaders. Believing that you can accept favors, like complimentary golf games on prestigious golf courses, and still maintain your objectivity can lead you to make choices that end up being less than admirable.

You've heard the age-old question "If a tree falls in a forest and no one is there to hear it, does it still make a sound?" If you quietly appoint a qualified relative to a job that needs to be filled and no one knows, is it unethical? One way to evaluate that question is to ask yourself if you would want it reported on the front page of the local newspaper. Actions that are ethical stand up to public scrutiny. If you prefer to keep your actions "under wraps," it's a good signal that perhaps you are making the wrong choices.

POLITICS AND ETHICS

The intersection of politics and ethics presents a thorny problem. You can pursue politics without a thought to ethics, and the choice of strategy and direction is a relatively easy one. But if you are committed to seeking a course of action that considers the ethics of the situation, it is a far more complex choice. Figure 6.2 displays the intersection of ethics, politics, and organizational interests.

Some decisions are political in nature and organizational in interest but not ethical in effect. A decision, such as whether or not to change the company dress code, is one example. It surely has political implications on satisfaction and productivity; it has organizational interest because it involves people's preferences and the image of the organization, but there are no ethical implications. It doesn't weigh good against evil or right against wrong.

On the other hand, there are a myriad of decisions that are both political and ethical in nature. For instance, whether or not to drill for oil in the North Coast of Alaska is surely political in nature. People are demanding "homegrown" oil instead of foreign oil. Others believe that drilling will damage the environment. It is ethical in nature because of the potential ecological impact. This combination of ethics and politics creates a crucial dynamic for the leader who is charged with decision making.

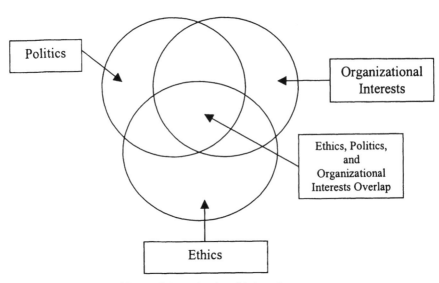

Figure 6.2   Politics, Ethics, and Organizational Interests

Another example is the decision of where to build a new school in a growing district. On its surface, it seems neither political nor ethical. But it can be both. In this example, parents in the growing area are paying extra facilities taxes and want the new school in their development. They are, by the way, a wealthy and predominantly white neighborhood with connections to elected officials in town. Another neighborhood wants the school in their older part of town where new families have moved in, some sharing dwellings, and a burgeoning number of children have enrolled in the neighborhood school. Parents here want the school to ease overcrowding and to give their children access to new technology and more state-of-the-art features. Their neighborhood is predominantly black.

An external political conflict is brewing, but also an ethical one. Do you integrate the school? Do you build it in the older part of town and bus people from the new development against their will? Do you acquiesce to de facto segregation by building the school in the all-white area of town? Do you give more assets to the privileged at the expense of those not so privileged? This is truly an ethical dilemma.

So you can see from the examples above that many organizational decisions have both a political dimension and an ethical one. The politically ethical leader must examine these dimensions and then act accordingly.

ETHICAL REFLECTIONS FOR
POLITICALLY INTELLIGENT LEADERS

If there is an ethical dimension involved in a decision, you must reflect on four questions:

1. What Are My Values?

First of all, you have to know your own values, both as a person and as a leader. You must record them and reflect upon them. On a sheet of paper, write your personal values. Reflect on these. Is honesty really a value to you? Is helping others a value you truly hold, or do you hold it only when it is easy to do so? Be brutally honest with yourself. Perhaps being parsimonious is a value of yours that you don't necessarily own up to. You might prefer to be thought of as generous, but what do your actions tell you? Promoting your self-interest may be more prevalent in your behavior than you'd prefer to admit. Reflect upon all your values—good and bad alike—and then rank them. Which ones come first? It's important to take this step because values often come into conflict with one another; and when they do, you need to be aware of which ones should take precedence. For instance, you have a dear friend. To tell him that the quality of his work is not up to organizational standards would deeply hurt his feelings, but you believe in honesty at all costs. Would you tell him or not? Does your belief in honesty outweigh your belief in protecting the feelings of a friend? By ranking your values and reflecting on them, you're better able to answer that difficult question.

Another important consideration in this reflection is to be aware of the values you believe you have and those that you project. Do they vary based on the situation, or are they constant? For example, in the case described above about where to place a new school, do you value the integration of races, or is neighborhood sovereignty more important to you? Do you hold one of these values dear but project, in practice, another? Is it situational?

These are all questions to reflect upon as you determine the answers for yourself. There is no set of right answers. Some answers are more aligned with your universal ethical principles and your values than others. Searching for that alignment is what makes these questions so difficult.

2. Are My Values Consistent with Good Ethical Principles?

Earlier, we identified honesty, integrity, trust, fairness, equity, and justice as Stephen Covey's suggestions for bedrock ethical principles. Individuals each have their own values—those ideals that guide their behavior. You have written and ranked your values in question 1. But how do those values line up with Covey's or other universal ethical principles that you may select?

For example, if honesty is your guiding ethical principle, then straightforward communication and an open, transparent decision-making process would be very compatible values. However, guarded communication is a value held by many leaders, and it plays out in hidden agendas or secrecy in plans and intentions. Providing selected facts to a selected few is not a value that is compatible with honest leadership unless you are talking about protecting patents, military maneuvers, or legitimate secrets that could harm your organization or its people if revealed.

If your ethical principle is integrity, do you value perseverance, or do you vacillate in the face of intimidation? Are you steadfast in pursuing the best interests of the organization? If not, you may come across as unpredictable in your decisions and policies. A person of integrity is a rock of reliability. She is unwavering in her commitment to the organization's vision and values. Integrity is the cornerstone of credibility. Without credibility, a leader will have few followers.

If you are guided by the ethical principle of trust, you say what you mean, mean what you say, and do what you promise. Your values would include sincerity and authenticity in the way you conduct business for your organization. Your unpretentious self-confidence would inspire others to follow your lead. And your faith in others would be another value that would play out in empowerment of colleagues and shared decision making.

The ethical principle of fairness implies values such as even-handedness, balance, and open-mindedness. Your values would include objectivity and reasonableness. You would resist the temptation of bias in favor of those in power or those who can help you or hurt you, personally.

If equity is an ethical principle you prize, then your values may include impartiality in distributing resources such as time, people, money, facilities, materials, and services. If equity is part of your ethical framework, accepting responsibility for what happens to the less privileged and less powerful might be one of your values. If equity is an important ethical principle to you, respect would be one of your values. Respect for the customs, traditions, language, beliefs, and cultural norms of individuals and groups would be apparent in your actions.

The ethical principle of justice calls for values like lawfulness, legitimacy, and righteousness. It is doing the honorable thing for your organization and the people it serves. But many have the value of doing what is in the "letter of the law" as opposed to observing the spirit or intent of the law. As we've said earlier, legal does not necessarily mean just. Which value do your behaviors show that you have?

Values can easily get off track and separated from the bedrock ethical principles that should guide our actions and decisions. Asking yourself if your values and your ethical principles are aligned is an important part of being a politically ethical leader.

3. Are the Political Strategies I Have Chosen Consistent with My Values?

As you explore the many political strategies available to you in this book, ask yourself if the ones you select work in each unique situation and are consistent with the values and ethical principles that are important to you.

For example, collaboration, open-mindedness, and respect may be values that you believe are well aligned with the ethical principles of trust, fairness, and equity. Which political strategies will support your values and ethical principles? Building trust before conflict arises might be an important political strategy that would line up with your ethical principles and values. In building trust, are you affable, accessible, and approachable? Are your deeds consistent with your words? Trust building as a political strategy involves demonstrating your belief in the interdependence that must exist between you and your stakeholders. Collaboration means that you use the political strategy of extending trust to others as well.

In the example above, where two neighborhoods—one affluent and one impoverished—are competing for a new school, using the political strategy of including all sides is critical. Involving only the people who agree with your direction or the ones who are the power brokers in the community would be neither compatible with your values nor a smart political strategy. The disenfranchised will go from feeling hurt to being outraged in the bat of an eye. Nothing invites anger faster than disrespect. To ignore their input on a matter that affects them so greatly is to show disrespect. It is unfair, and it breaches their trust.

Once they are at the table, do you engage in open, honest dialogue on the topic, or do you structure the conversation to address only those questions that are "safe"? You must be open to their ideas because they will sense it immediately if you are listening but not "hearing" them.

In the midst of this conflict over resources, such as facilities and finances, an important political strategy would be to engage stakeholder representatives in problem solving. This is far more effective than just taking the expedient path of issuing a command decision and hoping the problem will blow over. Engage them in generating criteria to help select the right alternative.

As you consider your ethical principles, your values, and the political strategies together, it will help you to sort out those prickly problems and take the action that will be in the best interest of your organization and the people you serve.

4. Will I Be Serving My Own Self-Interest or the Goals of the Organization?

Robert Greenleaf, the father of Servant Leadership, reminds us that the servant leader is servant first. Admitting that it is a difficult role, Greenleaf offered this test:

> Do those served grow as persons? Do they while being served become healthier, wiser, freer, more autonomous, more likely themselves to become servants? And what is the effect on the least privileged in society; will they benefit, or, at least, not be further deprived? (1977, pp. 13–14)

Let's face it; balancing our own self-interest with the goals of the organization isn't always easy. Leadership is a dangerous business. Whatever our recommendation or decision, not everyone is going to praise us. Yet it's crucial that politically ethical leaders act in ways that are consistent with the values, mission, and vision of the organization. As a superintendent many years ago, I supported the closure of the elementary school serving my own neighborhood. It was the right ethical decision. However, after all these years, I still have neighbors who won't talk to me.

In the previously mentioned problem of where to build a new school, it will be the school board that will make the decision, but it will be the leader, the superintendent, who must make the recommendation that addresses the interests of the many district stakeholders while mirroring a clear ethical imperative.

Ethical authenticity requires leadership by example. The leader must be seen as part of the process that results in organizational values, mission, and vision. Stakeholders must see the leader placing the interests of the organization above his or her own.

This does not begin at the time a school needs to be built. Rather, it begins with our first day on the job in a leadership position. It needs to be a conscious part of our "digging the well."

Ethical leaders recognize that decision making that is authentically embedded in the organization may not always be agreed with but must be respected. At the point where you find your personal interests diverging from those of the organization, you have an important decision to reach. Do you stay and violate your own values, or do you move on to a new organization with which you are comfortable?

What would I do in the matter of building a new school? First, I would have been working with the school board from my first day on the job to formalize district values, goals, and vision, thus working to align agendas. I would make sure that they are referred to and used on a regular basis in our ongoing decision making. I would widely share district values, goals, and vision with employees and the community and stress with the board the importance of practicing them authentically.

With that background, I would strive to go slow to go fast. I need to make sure that I have done my homework. Considering long-term enrollment projections of each option, as well as its impact on student learning, transportation, and safety, are part of that homework. Formal and informal opportunities to interact with our stakeholders can offer not only valuable input but political scanning opportunities.

Ultimately, when the time comes for a recommendation, I must reflect on the adopted values, goals, and vision of the district before framing it and then guide the board in making a decision that seeks the greater good and is consistent with our ethical framework.

FINAL THOUGHTS

It is in these four questions of reflection that you can begin to examine the ethics of a political situation. Volumes have been written about ethics by those who have made it their life's work. We have included some of these in our list of references. We would encourage you to engage in more study and reflection on this important topic, for in elevating yourself, you inspire others to reach for noble goals through principled behavior. Posing and answering these four questions will start you on that path.

7

Dealing with Special Public Sector Groups

Politics isn't a four-letter word, but for many of us it may as well be. "Just playing politics" creates a negative picture in our minds. It's almost an American tradition to look at politics with suspicion. Yet when we dive into a dictionary and look up *politic*, we find that it is to be expedient, advisable, prudent, tactical, or wise.

National or state politics are often far enough away from our everyday life that we can ignore or forget them. However, when it comes to most public leadership roles, we're reminded that all politics are local. We ignore politics at our peril, and it's impossible to forget its impact on our leadership.

Why do we too often resist the need to be political? Perhaps it's that when people come together with different goals and beliefs, there is bound to be conflict, and many of us prefer to avoid it. It brings out emotions — many of them negative. Tim Ursiny (2003) gives one answer to why we tend to avoid conflict — fear. Fears of rejection, failure, anger, and loss of relationships are very real consequences of conflict in our minds. Yet, if we want to be leaders and survive, we must be politically intelligent. We can run, but we can't hide.

Often, we refer to something called "the community." Oh, if it were only true. Whether within the organization, or in a school district, college, or city, there are many communities comprising people with their own interests, goals, and beliefs. Political intelligence requires that we not only make ourselves aware of the different communities that make up our environment, but also that we be mindful of their interests and their real and potential impact on our leadership. We ignore them at our peril. Let's look at a few of the communities you might be dealing with.

OTHER PUBLIC AGENCIES

One of the agencies that school districts, colleges, and universities work with on a continuing basis is the city council, as well as various branches of city government. We all serve the same people. Our governing boards may well be elected by the same voters. Getting along should be easy, right? Well, that might be true when our needs, goals, and beliefs are similar, but often there are issues on which we can't agree. In today's antitax world, we often look upon one another as competitors for resources.

Consider the case of a school district faced with an extremely tight budget. Looking for creative solutions, it decided to pursue using part of an existing high school campus on which to build apartments. A lease arrangement would result in the building of the project without district money and the benefit of a regular income stream. District teachers would be given preference as tenants in renting the units. How could the city resist going along with such a reasonable project and agreeing to a rezoning? Guess again.

It may have been a no-cost item to the school district, but it certainly wasn't to the city. The city pointed out that it also faced the same antitax public and that the sewage treatment system in the community would be inadequate, requiring extensive expenditures, not to mention traffic signals and the like. To do this would require negotiations with the county. Their answer was, "No way!" Rezoning would never get to first base. The initial anger on the part of the district gave way to the realization that it would have to become politically intelligent. Back to the drawing board.

Instead of conducting a campaign of pressure and rancor, sure to make matters worse, the district explored with the city staff its interests and openly shared the interests of the school district. By slightly redesigning the parcel in question, the city agreed to allow it to be rezoned for commercial use. While it was not quite as financially attractive to the district, the long-term lease would give it a sizable income while providing the city with a significant sales tax source. The sewage issue would no longer exist, and the income would help to offset the installation of new traffic signals and left-turn lanes. The property was leased to a large home improvement center which also provided part-time employment to students and staff.

In today's increasingly urbanized and suburbanized world, the potential for interagency conflict is very real. As Fisher and Ury (1988, p. 22) remind us, "Understanding the other side's thinking is not simply a useful activity that will help you solve your problem. Their thinking *is* the problem. Whether you are making a deal or settling a dispute, differences are defined by the difference in your thinking and theirs." Doing this takes time to listen and to understand the interests of the involved parties.

Kathleen Kelley Reardon (2001) reminds us of the importance of building relationships in becoming politically intelligent. The politically intelligent leader doesn't wait until there's a problem to develop relationships. It isn't enough to just interact with leaders of other agencies at service club meetings, as important as that may be. An ongoing effort to understand issues facing other agencies can be invaluable. Regular interaction builds mutual trust and appreciation of the leader's competency. Through relationships comes understanding. Through understanding comes mutual problem solving.

UNIONS

Perhaps no other community group calls for more of the leader's political intelligence than unions in the public sector. While the impact of unions in the private sector has declined in recent years, just the opposite is true in the public sector. Unions are not going away, and by now, you know they have political power.

It is imperative for the politically intelligent leader to accept the union as a legitimate community group. With acceptance comes mutual respect and the building of relationships that result in mutual problem solving.

Some leaders fool themselves by believing that employees do not really support their unions or their leadership. Remember, when conflict arises, employees will support the union. It is imperative that whether dealing with an officer of the union or a building representative, you have a responsibility to build an ongoing cordial relationship.

The politically intelligent superintendent does not ignore the union president, leaving the relationship to the human resources executive. A wise superintendent meets once a week with the president of the teachers union just to talk. They have a mutual agreement not to discuss issues that are topics in current negotiations and to keep discussions confidential unless there is mutual agreement. Instead, it's a time to build relationships and trust, and to discuss potential problems. Heading off potential problems makes life easier for both leaders. This doesn't mean that you seek to be friends, but neither should you be adversaries. Either relationship can be unhealthy. A cordial, professional, and sincere rapport is to the advantage of both parties.

It is important that the educational leader understand that the local union, while being an important local community group, is part of a larger community. The local chapter is part of regional, state, and national professional communities. The local union president is not only responsible to the chapter membership but to the goals and beliefs of the larger affiliates. Often, the pressure on the union president is intense. Politically intelligent superintendents, through active listening, seek to understand where the union president is coming from.

The politically intelligent leader works to make sure that the behavior of all members of the management team is consistent with the need to be cordial, professional, and sincere in union relationships—even when the favor isn't returned.

VOLUNTEER GROUPS

Volunteers are an important part of the picture whether at the school, district, university, or city level. Too often, we take their service for granted and make assumptions about them. We assume, because they provide us with support, that they automatically agree with our goals, beliefs, and needs—in fact, that they know what they are. Because of this, we may be guilty of a lack of attention to their needs and concerns and a lack of understanding of their political position and power.

The politically intelligent high school principal knows that the financial support provided by the football boosters is considerable. She also knows that it is one of the communities that she has to understand. Groups that provide large amounts of money to the school may expect their voices to be more influential on policy matters than is sometimes helpful, reasonable, or appropriate.

The principal can't just leave it up to one of her coadministrators to communicate with the group. She must be a participant in the communication process, making certain that the boosters understand the goals, beliefs, and needs of the school and the district. At the same time, she needs to listen to those in the group and to work with its leaders to make sure that she understands their needs and concerns. She needs to build trust with them and work to meet their needs to the extent possible. She must keep the information lines open and flowing both ways.

Digging the well early strengthens relationships during the good times and will help her to survive the tough times. As an example, if the principal is faced with a coach whose behavior is repeatedly inappropriate with students and fails to abide by directives to conform to district professional standards and codes of conduct, she may need to replace him or her. This can be an extremely difficult political decision, especially when the coach is popular in the school and community.

In such situations, principals are handicapped by the need to recognize the coach's right to privacy. A principal who has not built a trusting relationship with booster club members over the years can face daunting political conflict. It is important to remember MBWA—management by walking around—as a regular practice. Being visible at practices, games, and awards dinners gives the principal opportunities to interact with parents of players. This interaction helps the principal build trust with the community so that she will be given the benefit of the doubt when the community can't be privy to all the information.

The politically intelligent university president realizes that the fiscal advisory committee, composed of volunteers, will be focused on its own goals, beliefs, and needs, perhaps to the exclusion of those of the school. Clarifying the mission of the committee and collaboratively developing norms to guide their work together will help to set them on the right course. The president must see to it that he is also a teacher who educates the community as well as being an active listener. Listening to their interests will help him develop win-win solutions in times of scarce resources and mounting needs. The goals and beliefs of the advisory group must be compatible with those of the university. Failure to bring this about may result in political conflict as the advisory group arrives at its recommendations. Continuing dialogue and a willingness to think outside the box is usually appreciated by advisory groups who often see us as "traditional bureaucrats" lacking creative ideas and unwilling to try something new. Looking for ways to "expand the pie" can earn their respect and trust even when the solutions are not what they were hoping for.

The politically intelligent city administrator is no less challenged when dealing with the city's many commissions and advisory groups, each with its own sense of community. Through communication and active listening, she maximizes the degree to which the different communities share goals and beliefs. Working with commission members is complicated because of their individual relationships with city council members who often appoint them. This can create a dynamic in which "end runs" around the city administrator by appointer and appointee become routine. The city administrator with political intelligence is going to find it easier to keep her priorities straight.

Political blind spots can abound in situations like this. Surfacing connections, defining personal agendas, and knowing who trusts whom can be very helpful in this politically active environment.

The elementary principal who assumes that the beliefs and goals of the PTA charter automatically agree with those of the school and district has a need to develop a greater degree of political intelligence. It's hard work, but by recognizing that politics play a significant role in ultimately making her job more pleasant, she will develop trust and help both the PTA and the school achieve their goals.

The politically intelligent leader realizes that volunteers are often the future school board members and council members with whom he or she will work. It is never too early to build important relationships and develop understanding. Volunteer groups appreciate the personal attention of the leader. They like to be "in the know" about what's going on now and what's going to happen in the future. Communication is vitally important. Involving them in decisions helps to gain their support. Floating ideas with this group will serve as a useful barometer in forecasting public support for changes.

ELECTED AND APPOINTED OFFICIALS

We don't have to remind you of the importance of internal politics. You experience them every day. For superintendents and city administrators, being politically intelligent is crucial as they deal with their governing bodies. Survival depends on it.

Each governing board member comes to the job with personal goals and beliefs about the leader and the organization. They often come with a set of issues and needs for which they either believe they have the answer or that they think they can motivate the organization to solve. They have a constituency to which they feel some allegiance. The politically intelligent leader knows that he somehow must help every new governing board member become a meaningful part of the district leadership team.

Looking at the governing board solely as a body would be a big mistake. It really is a group of individuals with whom the leader needs to develop a relationship. Discovering their individual goals and beliefs is crucial to linking agendas and building trust. Being open to individual perspectives develops mutual respect. We're not suggesting that the leader should waffle on issues because of relationships. The board expects the leader to make tough decisions and to provide guidance with quality recommendations even when these might disappoint individual members.

The leader has a responsibility to help the board meld its individual preferences into a set of goals and beliefs that lead to a common vision. However, stepping on the toes of individual elected officials can have consequences, and it's important to use diplomacy and excellent communication skills in working with them. Digging the well before you're thirsty becomes an extremely valuable strategy at times like this. Building relationships that can withstand diverse opinions makes all the difference in both professional success and a pleasant working environment.

All of this means that the leader has to be a constant planner. You can't just let things happen. We're not talking about manipulation. We're talking about ethically getting things done in a manner that is consistent with the board's vision and goals. This means doing your homework regularly and consistently.

While developing a relationship with individual board members, the leader needs to avoid the impression that he is in the pocket of any one of them. Equal treatment, attention, and communication build mutual trust, a crucial tool for the politically intelligent leader. A great motto for the leader and the board is "No surprises."

Dealing with external elected officials is a challenge for the leader. Elected officials, regardless of whether they represent the school district, city, county, or state, prefer to deal with other elected officials. Often there is competition between governing bodies and their individual members. There is generally an expectation that staff members should deal with one another on issues rather than directly approaching external elected officials. That should not prevent the leader from developing a respectful but affable relationship with elected officials from external boards and councils. Being perceived as an effective leader by elected officials of other entities is as desirable as by your own board. Learning which issues are important to other elected members and bodies can only result in mutual trust and help the leader develop political strategies that encourage interdependence.

We pointed out above that the preference of our own elected officials and those of other agencies is that we deal with staff members rather than directly with those from other agencies. This means that there is a need for us to develop a relationship with their staffs, particularly before situations that could end in conflict.

Stephen Covey's Habit 5, *seek first to understand, then to be understood* (1989) should guide us. It's important for us to be able to convey the needs of our organization to other elected agencies, particularly when the journey goes through their appointed officials. This means we need to have developed a cordial relationship with them built on mutual understanding. Any solid relationship takes time to develop, to overcome the suspicion of competition, and to achieve respect for our leadership. Our openness to other agencies' needs, goals, and beliefs can only improve interagency cooperation. Waiting until there is conflict will make our desire to be understood more difficult. Regular informal meetings with our counterparts before conflict occurs builds empathy. Keep in mind, while informality is a step in mutual understanding, it's important to know when confidentiality is called for.

Foundations

We've already mentioned that we are seeing more financial dependence on booster clubs, with an accompanying need to be politically intelligent.

More and more universities, schools, and districts are becoming involved with foundations, both internal and external. Generally, these are groups that focus more on supporting the academic program.

Some of the caveats previously mentioned about booster clubs also pertain to internal foundations. There is a crucial need for the leader to make certain that internal foundations understand the needs, goals, vision, and beliefs of the organization and that its goals are consistent with those of the district or college. Their intentions are uniformly good, but the need to avoid conflict is important. This requires ongoing communication and monitoring. Governing boards expect us to make sure that foundations understand the role of elected officials and their obligations to the organization.

On occasion, a foundation may be faced with donors who want their donation to support a specific program. That program may not be one that the organization can or wants to support. This presents a potential political conflict requiring skillful strategy. Being proactive is essential. Norms for working together need to be developed ahead of time. Set criteria for accepting donations in advance of fund-raising. Failure to do this risks certain conflict. It is then when conflict resolution strategies such as dialogue, problem solving, compromise, and smoothing may help you resolve any impasse that occurs.

External foundations provide additional challenges. Typically, it is harder for the leader to have an impact on mutual understanding. External foundations are often located a distance away from our locale. Their governance structure is such that we may not even know who members of their board are. We know who our staff counterpart is, but geography may make it difficult for us to develop a relationship.

We need to first make sure we aren't blinded by possible dollars without investigating the foundation's goals, vision, and beliefs. Care needs to be taken to find out from where the foundation gets its money and who its supporters are. Better to do that before an application is made rather than to be embarrassed later.

Monitoring the external foundation is just as important as with internal foundations. Because the governance structure of external foundations and their decisions are less transparent to us, we need to monitor them. Changes in their policies may result in conflict with ours.

FINAL THOUGHTS

As we've said before, politics can be satisfying, but it takes work. When dealing with both internal and external communities, we have to both build relationships and constantly monitor them. Making assumptions about the degree to which our goals, vision, beliefs, and needs are the same is dangerous.

The politically intelligent leader knows that both internal and external politics are a legitimate part of the job. To ignore either will result in unnecessary conflict. The protocol for dealing with each community described here requires an effort to understand their political needs, and regular communication to help them understand those of the organization.

While internal communities may be closer to us, external communities also have an effect on our organizational leadership. If we are unwilling to reach out to both internal and external communities, we cannot be called politically intelligent. If this is the case, we need to examine our ability to lead the organization.

Finally, we need to remember that we have a responsibility to both our organization and its governing board. The perceptions of others about our competence and ethics are reality to them, and that reality impacts our ability to successfully lead our organization and attend to the goals of our governing board.

8

Digging Your Way Out of a Political Hole

LEADERSHIP IS DANGEROUS

There has recently been a change of leadership in an organization. The new CEO decides that it might be wise to seek advice from the recently deposed chief. The newbie asks what the former CEO would advise her to do to respond to very serious mistakes that she might make. The response is a long pause after which he reaches in his desk, pulls out three envelopes, and hands them to her. "When you make the first big mistake, open envelope number one. When you make the next big mistake, open envelope number two. Of course, when you make the third blunder, open envelope number three. That should take care of things."

Later when the new CEO makes her first big mistake, she remembers the envelopes in the bottom drawer of her desk and opens number one. She unfolds the paper and reads, "Blame it on your predecessor." Time passes and the CEO makes another significant mistake. Once again, she remembers the envelopes and opens number two, which says, "Blame it on subordinates." Still much later, the CEO realizes that she has made yet another serious mistake. She recalls the third envelope, opens it, and reads, "Prepare three envelopes."

Yes, leadership is a dangerous business. There are consequences for leaders who make mistakes, and not all of them need to be large mistakes. Many leaders who have lost their jobs say they didn't see it coming.

As we look at successful leaders, we see people possessing vision, managerial skill, effective human relations, and political intelligence. By being politically intelligent, we have a better chance of surviving as leaders. Political intelligence in itself won't compensate for a lack of vision, managerial ability, or tacky human relations skills, but if we practice it reflectively, we can actually add quality to the other three elements. In baseball, managers often say that pitching is 70 percent of the game. In the game of leadership, political intelligence is just as significant.

LEADER POWERLESSNESS

Leaders can become powerless when faced with the realities of the tale of three envelopes. In *Confidence*, Rosabeth Moss Kanter (2004) describes nine pathologies when organizational problems arise and the leader feels powerless to solve them (pp. 97–98):

1. Communication decreases.
2. Criticism and blame increase.
3. Respect decreases.
4. Isolation increases.
5. Focus turns inward.
6. Rifts widen and inequities grow.
7. Initiative decreases.
8. Aspirations diminish.
9. Negativity spreads.

These all can have a negative impact on the confidence people have in their leadership, not to mention organizational morale. Accountability, initiative, and collaboration take a hit. People feel powerless. Every organization experiences some degree of powerlessness at one time or another. We don't have enough money to do what we would like to make the vision a reality, people may not feel valued, and resentment toward the leader may further erode leadership effectiveness. The problem is that we often don't see powerlessness blossoming. This is where political intelligence has to play a role.

Del had been a city manager in Center City for seven years. He enjoyed his time there and had been regarded as a highly effective leader. For six of the seven years, he had the same five members of the city council who had been overwhelmingly supportive. It had been Del's practice to send a confidential letter to the council with other information each Friday. He frequently pointed out the sensitivity of the letter, and members had kept its contents confidential.

Last fall, one of the council members retired, and a new person was elected. Del made every effort to continue the confidentiality of the Friday letter. Some months later, Del mentioned concerns about one of the employees in the letter. A few days later, that employee came to him to share that the new council member had shown him the letter with the negative comments. He thought Del should know.

Del determined that he did not want to create disharmony on the council, so he decided to stop sharing personnel items in his Friday letter. Del also discovered that some confidential items that were discussed in department head meetings were being shared with the new council member, who then challenged Del privately and publicly with the information. Despite his cautions to department heads, the problem persisted. Del began to feel anger and resentment. He decided to limit discussions of issues in department head meetings and to share these sensitive issues only with the assistant city manager.

After a time, Del received a critical review from the council citing a lack of sufficient information on personnel issues. Department heads also became resentful because they felt that they were being deprived of information necessary for them to make knowledgeable decisions. A notable lack of trust was permeating the organization and affecting Del's ability to lead.

WHEN YOU'RE IN A POLITICAL HOLE

While we can empathize with Del and his political problems, we can all have suggestions for him, most of which go back to the start of his digging a hole for himself. Sad to say, there is no recipe for digging ourselves out of a political hole. Talk about variables! Even with a helpful list, the leader who finds himself in a hole is going to have to *reflect, respond,* and perhaps *react* to his dilemma based upon analysis of the situation, good old common sense, political competence, and maybe lots of luck.

Reflecting

From Del's story, we're not sure of the degree of his reflection. Political conflict is often responded to by leaders with a rush to decision making. Oh sure, Malcolm Gladwell (2005) in his book *Blink* describes great decision makers as those who have perfected the art of filtering, or *thin slicing*, which he describes as "the ability of our unconscious to find patterns in situations and behavior based on very narrow slices of experience" (p. 23).

However, this thin slicing is something that few of us have perfected without lots of experience. A former secretary of state is said to have had a plaque on his desk that said, "Don't just do something—stand there." When faced with a political problem, it is time to reflect before we act.

Let's look at seven strategies of reflection.

1. Don't Rely on What's Worked Before

While it is certainly true that experience is a great teacher, we need to remember that just as in football, variables change. The opposing coach mixes the defensive alignment, and the quarterback understands that he must be ready to respond to it at the line of scrimmage. Del had been a successful and experienced city manager who was faced with challenges he had not previously experienced. Perhaps he assumed that the playing field really had not changed with the election and that the old plays would work.

Every political conflict we face has new wrinkles to it. Assuming that what worked yesterday addressing a similar problem will work with today's challenge is potentially dangerous. Our experience will be a useful reference, but we need to reflect on the uniqueness of each situation we face. Avoiding assumptions will contribute to our political intelligence.

2. Analyze Culture and Context

Organizational culture, even in mature systems, is constantly undergoing change. Sometimes we become so absorbed in the everyday operation of the job of leadership that we don't see it changing. We assume—there's that word again—that there is constancy in the organization and that we can rely upon others to keep it so. However, people in our organizations change, both in fact and in beliefs. Del didn't see the changing chemistry in his organization. Just one new person on the city council had an enormous impact on the culture of the organization.

A politically intelligent leader knows that he must constantly assess how the organization is changing. Hands-on leadership must be a constant and consistent practice. Visibility in the organization, rather than relying solely on immediate subordinate managers for input, is a must. Perhaps if Del had spent more of his time managing by walking around and listening, he might have seen what was happening in the organization.

3. Go to the Balcony

In *Leadership on the Line*, Heifetz and Linsky (2002) suggest the importance of this technique in better understanding the culture of the organization. They use going to the balcony metaphorically, suggesting that if we attend a dance and remain on the floor, we see only the dynamics of those who are close by. We cannot see what is going on beyond our close environment. However, if we go up to the balcony and look down on the dancers, we see much more. The interaction, or its lack, among individuals and groups can be observed. It is important to take time, stand back, and get a perspective on the way things are.

The practice of not only spending time on the floor but also going to the balcony provides perspective on a changing organizational culture. While the balcony is figurative, taking the time to interact with different groups and individuals within the organization and regularly reflecting upon what we discover can reveal and hopefully diminish the number of surprises that lead to political conflict and its consequences.

4. Identify Your Emotions and Think through How They Are Impacting Your Decisions and Actions

Daniel Goleman and his colleagues (2002) remind us of the importance of self-awareness as the first step in achieving emotional intelligence. It is imperative that we have a realistic understanding of our emotions, strengths, limitations, and values.

Emotions are natural but are not always helpful in facing our problems. Hubris has been the downfall of many leaders. Assuming that there is only one way of solving problems or applying motives to the actions of others can create political dysfunction. Del may not have been aware of his own emotions as he dealt, or did not deal, with his new council member. Perhaps he assumed that only he was right in the operation of the city because things had always gone fine before. Maybe he subconsciously downgraded what he felt the beliefs of the new council member were because of the new person's lack of experience. Perhaps he just didn't like the new member.

Anger is a natural and necessary emotion, but when we act precipitously in response, anger can be dangerous. No one really likes to be disagreed with, particularly when it comes from a source that is ill informed or is using power. Each of us has a limit to which we tolerate disagreement. Being self-aware of those limits is important to political competency. Our limits may differ when dealing with different individuals or different situations.

How we respond to our anger is the important thing. Taking the advice of the secretary of state, "Don't just do something—stand there," makes a great deal of sense—reflect. Del needed to think about his emotions and those of others. He needed to work from his head—not his gut.

Emotions, then, do impact our decisions and actions. Being constantly self-aware of them can aid in the development of our political intelligence.

5. Change Victim Stories into Anecdotal Accounts and Analyze Your Role in the Problem

It is easy to believe that we are a victim of circumstances or of another person's actions. In fact it may be true, but playing the role of the victim adds nothing to leadership effectiveness. When we focus on being a victim, we begin to think as one, and we lose the ability for self-awareness. This is particularly the case when we share our feelings with subordinates. Our complaints about our superiors will undoubtedly make their way back to them in time, adding to our political dilemma.

It is during these times of feeling powerless that we need to reflect on what role we might be playing that leads us and others to believe that we are victims, and to plan our strategy to change things.

There is a tendency for some who believe they are victims to become withdrawn and invisible. The lack of visibility only adds to our sense of powerlessness and to others' belief that we are indeed a victim and that our leadership is in jeopardy. When you are in political jeopardy, this is the time to be highly visible rather than invisible. You need to gain perspective about the situation you are in and to establish yourself as strong in the perceptions of others. Under pressure, Del retreated and chose only to interact with the assistant city manager, and in doing so he only added to his isolation.

6. Seek the Counsel of a Trusted Adviser

There was no evidence that Del asked anyone to listen to his situation, let alone that he tried to get advice. This is often a mistake that leaders make. Ego gets in the way of common sense. We are in charge of an organization. We may believe that we should not admit that we have a problem in carrying out our duties and in handling political conflict. Instead, we need a trusted person with whom we can confide our inadequacies, and from whom we can seek perspective and advice. We can only gain understanding of the issue by talking it out with someone we trust.

In doing so, however, we need to proceed with caution. Heifetz and Linsky (2002) remind us of the difference between "allies" and "confidants." The former individuals are those with whom we have rapport but who may be conflicted by our request that a matter be held in confidence. The latter, often outside our organization, can provide us with the confidentiality and objectivity that we need.

Often just describing our predicament to a trusted confidant results in our discovering our own solution. That trusted confidant may be a trained executive coach. These individuals may often be reached through professional organizations or universities. Their services can be tailor made at a reasonable cost. Remember, no one person has all the answers.

7. Separate "Facts" from Fiction

When we describe what we see or hear about a problem to subordinates or superiors without considering what Jim Collins (2001) calls "the brutal facts" and our role in making them what they are, we run the risk of making the problem worse. When we take time to ask questions and dialogue on the issue, we are more likely to reach objectivity, and our actions will more often be the appropriate ones.

Fisher and Ury (1988), in their classic *Getting to Yes*, remind us of the importance of separating the people from the problem. By understanding that there is danger in focusing on people rather than the problem, ego may become the motivator of inappropriate behavior on our part. Great care needs to be taken in what we say. Once said, words cannot be erased.

In the scenario, there was no evidence that Del sought to clarify the position or intentions of the new council member, and so he defined them without separating fact from fiction.

Responding

The previous section emphasized the importance of reflection and self-awareness. In this section, we consider nine strategies in helping us to dig our way out of political conflict. Reflection and self-awareness without action do little to resolve political conflict. In our scenario, Del labored over his situation but did little to solve it productively. Let's consider these strategies.

1. Take Charge of Your Body Language

We can find a bookcase of texts on the "silent language" that have been written through the years. A common thread among them is that our body language is more important than what we say. The positions of the head, arms, and hands join our facial expressions in communicating our thoughts and intentions to others.

We don't know from the scenario what role the "silent language" had in Del's political conflict. We do know that people who come under intense pressure may be able to control what they say and how they say it, but they often have difficulty controlling nonverbal communication.

One's posture may reflect low self-esteem by slumping in the chair. Failure to maintain eye contact may be interpreted as a lack of interest, trust, or respect. It is during difficult times like this that our grooming may slip as well.

By striving to present a self-assured and cheerful disposition at all times, our words and body language tend to reflect the same demeanor. An erect posture reflects confidence, a crucial ingredient in what people want to see in a leader.

Consultant Art Lustberg (1984) reminds us that an open and animated face can help us to get our point across. When we are confronted, we close the muscles in our head, creating a frown line that we believe is professional but that others may interpret as pomposity or coldness. Simply raising our eyebrows can create a face that reflects warmth and openness. It sends the message that we are a confident and strong leader and slows attackers down.

Taking charge of the "silent language" is crucial, particularly when involved in potential or real political conflict. Not to do so may add to the perception of victimization and questions about our leadership effectiveness.

2. Avoid the Blame Game: Take Responsibility

It never rains but it pours. It seems that problems come in bunches rather than one at a time. Subordinates can let us down. Understandably, unanticipated problems can arise. It is an unfortunate fact that people will want to know "who is responsible."

It's too easy to blame someone or something else for our problems. When we take responsibility and describe remedies, we suddenly get people on our side. When we sincerely accept vulnerability, others will approach us with understanding and empathy.

Of course, we must take care to see that, as Jim Collins (2001) calls it, the organization has the "right people on the bus." However, it is inappropriate when things go wrong to pin the tail on someone or something else. After all, we are the leader and are responsible for what goes on in our organization.

It is tough to admit that the organization with you at its head made a mistake. Taking responsibility, and perhaps more importantly, presenting a plan to see that the problem doesn't reoccur, is the appropriate role for the leader.

3. Work on Yourself First: Develop Your Own Patience, Courage, Strength, and Grace

I am upset, not by events, but rather by the way I view them.

Epictetus

We've all heard the old saying "Patience is a virtue." Indeed it
is. It leads to the trust of those whom we lead. It is one of the
first traits that subordinates mention when asked to describe an
effective leader. For most of us, it is not a natural trait. Once a
goal is in mind, we want to get there—fast. That is one reason
why we are leaders. Balancing patience with achievement is a
lifelong pursuit.

As hard as it may be sometimes to be patient with subordinates, it is
most difficult for leaders to be patient with themselves. Seeking self-
awareness of one's level of patience in dealing with conflict is a key to
leadership success. However, patience is not just enduring and waiting for
things to happen. Rather, it is an active state in which we continue to focus on the goal but are constantly seeking alternative routes on the way.

It has been said that courage is not without fear, but it is fearlessly doing the right thing. Easier said than done. Councils and boards of trustees
are composed of individuals who bring different agendas that often are in
conflict not only with the other governing board members but with the vision and mission of the organization. Preferences rather than principles
may rule the day.

It takes courage for the leader to make principled recommendations that
violate governing board member preferences. We pay a price for it, but it
is part of the job.

One definition of strength is "the power to resist strain or stress; dura-
bility" (*American Heritage Dictionary*, 2001, p. 813). We are familiar
with the role that exercise and diet have in the development of physical
strength, although we sometimes forget to make it a regular part of our
lives. Just as important to our success in developing political intelligence
is the development of emotional strength.

Striving to get in the habit of being aware of our own emotional state is
an important contribution to our political intelligence. Taking a moment
to consider our emotions, particularly in difficult times when faced with
having to select strategy, is just smart. We need to consider the impact that
others have on our emotional state. Individuals and groups affect us in different ways. Awareness of the emotional state of individuals with whom
we come in contact is crucial. The temptation to respond to anger with
anger is a natural reaction. Being aware of the fact that we just may not

care for an individual can save us from behavior that results in a political problem.

Self-awareness is fine, but then we have to manage the situation. Taking responsibility for our part in interactions and events plays a role in developing our emotional strength. Avoiding actions or comments that do not help the situation requires strength. Being in control of our emotions and behaviors adds credibility to our leadership in the eyes of others. When others cannot get our goat, there is greater likelihood that they will respect our leadership and respond in kind.

Developing grace is directly connected with awareness and management of our emotions. Recognition that there will be tough times in our career and that we have choices in responding to them is an important part of achieving grace. Defining for ourselves the principles and goals that we hold important is another part in achieving grace.

Approaching difficult situations as opportunities to learn helps to control our emotions and behaviors. Grace, then, is a condition far more complicated than merely accepting conditions we find ourselves facing. It requires self-awareness and a conscious intellectual decision to learn from the challenges that we meet.

4. Write Down Your Priorities—Identify Your "Hills to Die On"

It is important to (a) know what our personal priorities are, (b) write them on a list, and (c) ask to what degree we are living out our values and priorities. By doing this on a regular basis, we can see to what degree our behavior is consistent with our values and priorities rather than based only on preferences or a desire to get even.

A word of advice: review the priority list often. New challenges arise and old ones fall off the table. We want to spend our political capital on those issues that are in the best interests of the organization. Clinging to outdated priorities places our leadership in jeopardy.

5. Focus Attention on the Issue and Solutions

As difficult as it may be, we must turn the attention of stakeholders away from the "blame game." Instead, concentrate organizational attention on the issue to be resolved and its solutions. Making excuses only presents questions about our leadership.

Certainly, accountability must be attended to, but the importance of positive problem solving must be modeled and made a part of the organization's culture. The "blame game" wastes emotion and energy that can better be used on solving issues. Trust is damaged, and along with it, creativity.

6. Communication Is Crucial and Must Be Planned Carefully

Communication is the mother's milk of an effective organization. As stated earlier, our bosses rarely feel that they have all the information that we know about an issue. In the case of governing boards, some members are often sure that everyone else on the board is getting information that they are not. The same can be said about subordinates who value a confidential relationship with their boss.

The politically intelligent leader must establish and maintain a culture of communication as a keystone. This communication culture needs to exist in good times and bad. Indeed, it is in the good times that the culture becomes established so that tough issues are kept in context.

The method of communication is also a factor. When pressure arises, we need to avoid not only cutting the quantity but changes in the method. Del decided to limit communication, first to the council and then to the staff. It is tempting to hold back communication during the tough times, but this is just the wrong thing to do. There is a temptation for us to reduce face-to-face contacts and to rely principally on the written word, or worse, on e-mail. Perhaps the advice of then New York State attorney general Eliot Spitzer—"Never write when you can talk. Never talk when you can nod. And never anything in an e-mail"—may be overly cynical, but there is a lot of truth in it (Spitzer, 2005, p. 114).

Yet effective communication, whether in good times or bad, requires truth along with political strategies that frame and focus the accomplishments and needs of the organization. Different audiences need a clear understanding of the message, which may require different strategies.

In our scenario, Del neglected communication and allowed others to develop their own understanding of the problem based upon what information they had. It probably cost him.

Building an effective and politically competent communication culture in which subordinates are free to express disagreement with our perspectives in an appropriate setting without fear of the consequences is imperative. Subordinates must feel free but obligated to share the bad along with the good with the leader. Members of the organization must understand their roles when it comes to a voice speaking for it.

Whenever or whatever, the essence of the message must be understood in the minds of all stakeholders of the organization. This requires reflection and the building of strategies to assure a politically viable and honest culture. It is during tough times that we need to avoid the careless off-the-cuff comment or the quickly sent e-mail. In the midst of crisis or controversy, it is wise to get feedback from a trusted confidant before reacting. Carefully planning all communication in times like this makes good sense.

There are occasions when the print medium takes exception to decisions that we make. The temptation to respond with indignation can be a temptation, but it is well to remember the old saw, "Never argue with someone who buys ink by the barrel and paper by the ton." It is far better to prepare a cordial face-to-face conversation with the writer or editor.

Writing letters, particularly in response to attack letters, can be dangerous. This is particularly so when the attack is unfair. It is tempting to respond in kind, but it is time for self-awareness and self-managing our emotions. It is time for a face-to-face personal contact. If you believe you must write an attack letter to vent, do so, but then tear it up.

7. Meet the Parties Face to Face

In our scenario, Del sought to avoid conflict by dismissing a face-to-face approach to resolving a festering issue. Perhaps he hoped that the problem would just go away. Maybe his self-confidence led him to believe that he would win over his unhappy council member. In either case, it usually doesn't happen, and political consequences are sure to result.

A school district superintendent who was faced with making deep and hurtful budget reductions, on the other hand, decided to spend a full day at each of the schools in face-to-face meetings with teachers and support staff. He shared the bad news, faced angry questions, and asked for suggestions. People throughout the organization heard the same message and had the same opportunity to express emotion and offer some helpful suggestions.

It was a humbling experience for the superintendent, but while resentment continued to exist in the organization, there were no surprises as to what would have to take place. The superintendent understood that it would be more difficult for folks to be angry with him or the school board because of the face-to-face visits. It would be much easier to be angry with an invisible person.

The practice of some leaders to make themselves scarce or to use representatives to avoid politically charged situations is risky and allows others to form incomplete or inaccurate pictures. At the same time, face-to-face meetings require careful preparation. The purpose for the meeting and possible strategies must be considered in order to assure success.

8. Send It to Committee for Further Study

This can be a legitimate strategy for some issues. It can put a hot potato in a cooler context, but beware. It can be perceived as an all-too-common strategy to tuck away discontent while actually avoiding a solution. It needs to be used only when there is a need to obtain meaningful input and when there is a clear intent to use it to deal with an issue. Forming a committee can result in more collaboration and input. To deal with natural suspicions, the meetings must normally be public and have its progress reported on an ongoing basis.

Not all issues lend themselves to this strategy. Certainly Del's political problem was highly personal in nature and required a personal response.

9. Listen More—Speak Less

Too often, we think of the importance of communication only in terms of giving our message. We forget the importance of the primary language: listening.

Leaders want to appear in charge, and getting others to listen to us is key to this image. This is what we want, sure, but frankly it is a politically dangerous want. It can reinforce a negativity that might foil what we wish to achieve.

Whether dealing with small or large problems, listening trumps speaking. In our scenario, it appears that not only did Del not speak at all, but he didn't listen either. People appreciate being heard, and that requires sincere and active listening. The case of the budget-harried superintendent attests to the value of listening.

A hospital administrator who prides herself on face-to-face contacts with unhappy staff, patients, and their family members is fully committed to the concept of listening more and speaking less. In her words,

> Many times, my administrative assistant has indicated that an individual wants to meet with me to complain about a particular issue or service. My practice is to start off such conferences by asking what they feel the problem is, and I write it on a white board that I have in my office where both of us can see it. It is amazing how often what I've been led to believe the problem to be turns out to be something totally different. Listening makes it possible for me to focus on the real problem. I also sometimes ask them to tell what solution would satisfy them. Often their solution is totally simple and reasonable.

Active listening is not only a strategy to gain rapport but a method by which to learn from others.

Reacting

Action has certainly been a part of the previous strategies, but there are times and situations when our careful consideration of them is no longer appropriate and we are faced with the final set of strategies—reacting.

1. Weather the Storm

President Harry Truman had a plaque on his desk that said, "The buck stops here." There are times when there is nothing to do but ride the riptide until you can get out of it. This requires courage and the willingness to assume responsibility. It doesn't mean surrendering our responsibilities as a leader or hiding out in our cave licking our wounds. It is a time to be visible and strong and to focus on helping others in the organization to survive the tsunami.

2. Retreat

Leaders don't make mistakes, do they? Of course they do, and people are surprisingly forgiving, providing it isn't a habit. President John F. Kennedy is a case in point. The Cuban Missile Crisis took place in 1962 after he had been office for just one year. A band of Cuban exiles were secretly supported by the U.S. government and were landed in Cuba only to be abandoned without air support. It was a great embarrassment to the president and the nation. Despite the warnings of internal political advisers, Mr. Kennedy went on television and admitted his role in the support of the invaders and apologized. Despite the political predictions of doom, Kennedy's public approval rating soared to 80 percent.

There may come a time when our conscience or common sense tells us that we were wrong or untimely and that we must retreat honorably. Doing so openly and humbly only strengthens our leadership.

3. Leave

Sometimes the political culture of an organization is such that an exit is the appropriate strategy. When we feel ethically conflicted because of the direction of the boss or governing board, or when we realize that our efficacy has been so compromised that we can no longer serve the needs of the organization, it may be time to leave.

When contemplating the loss of effectiveness, there may come a time when we need to decide upon leaving on our own terms or being fired. In the musical *Man of La Mancha*, Don Quixote's squire reminds him that whether the pitcher gets hit by the stone, or the stone gets hit by the pitcher, the results are the same. We may become the pitcher.

There are advantages in leaving gracefully on our own terms. It could be a time of reassessment and reflection. Is another position what you want? Remember that it could be a time to explore other career opportunities.

Fighting the decision of the boss to fire you is usually counterproductive. It can interfere with your ability to be considered for future job opportunities, and often any settlement is greatly diminished by attorney fees. Don't count on a public hue and cry either. It rarely works. In fact, although many will give you encouraging lip service privately, they are unlikely to stand up for you publicly. Most members of the public only know you casually and respect the right of the governing board to change leadership.

If possible, it's wise to stay alert that the end of your relationship with the organization may be on the horizon and plan for a transition to the next job while you are still holding your current position. It's always easier to find a job when you already have one. It's harder when you are unemployed. Negotiating the timing of your departure and elements of a separation agreement may be an option to consider if you are being terminated. Sometimes you may be able to discuss extension of health benefits for a period of time or some level of compensation, depending on the circumstances.

FINAL THOUGHTS

Our challenge is to respect the importance of politics in the operation of the organization and in our public leadership. Being politically intelligent is not an accident. It is the result of hard work. Being self-aware, reflective, and self-managing make up the foundation for political intelligence. Recognizing that politics are constantly changing and that selecting appropriate strategies for managing requires staying on top of what is happening within and without our organization. Remember, it is not just our survival as leaders that is at stake but an entire hospital, city, school, or college that suffers when its leadership becomes a revolving door.

IV

PULLING IT ALL TOGETHER

9

Practicing What We Preach

In this chapter, we want to afford you the opportunity to try out some of the strategies we have described in the foregoing chapters. In the three ensuing scenarios, we want you to answer seven questions.

1. Who are the key players?
2. What are their political styles?
3. What are their political connections?
4. What are the possible blind spots?
5. What special groups need attention?
6. What political strategies could be used to influence the outcome?
7. What potential ethical dilemmas exist?

After you have considered these questions relative to each scenario, you can turn to our analyses and compare your ideas to ours.

SCENARIO 1: SCHOOL CLOSURE—A POLITICAL NIGHTMARE

Superintendent Ellen Chavez, the leader in this scenario, has recommended to the board that the district close a school as part of a program of budget cuts. Upon being hired, the board indicated the need to close a school, but it has taken Superintendent Chavez two years to initiate the process. The board unanimously accepted the recommendation and authorized the formation of a School Closure Committee to listen to community input; to consider issues such as student safety, impact on instruction, and financial benefit to the district; and to recommend a specific school for closure.

Each board member selected one member of the community to serve along with representatives from staff, PTA, and a group of community volunteers. Dr. Bill Reynolds, a respected local physician, was selected as the chair. The committee has met weekly for the past two months and has been diligent in seeking public input and examining financial, safety, and instructional issues. Often the committee has had to endure public anger. The board has received the minutes of each committee meeting, and the process has been regularly reported by the local newspaper. During the process, Dr. Chavez and members of the board adhered to a "hands-off" policy, neither speaking with Dr. Reynolds nor with members of the committee.

Dr. Reynolds has provided masterful leadership as the committee's chair. His reputation as a person who understands group processes has been very much in evidence. Through the years, his leadership has been sought by service clubs, youth organizations, and city advisory committees because of his high ethical standards. He has emphasized the need to maintain an objective and open stance throughout the deliberations. As president of the chamber of commerce, he will have a significant influence on the reactions of the business and professional communities.

Two weeks ago at the board meeting, Dr. Reynolds reported that the school closure committee was unanimously recommending the closure of East Elementary School, which has the smallest enrollment and serves an affluent community. Superintendent Chavez expressed support for the recommendation, and the board shared its appreciation for the committee's efforts. The final decision was deferred to last night's school board meeting.

In a surprise move, Board Member Elaine Webb, whose child attends East Elementary School, moved to close, not the committee's recommended school, but West Elementary School, which serves largely Title I students and has the district's largest enrollment. The board member recommendation was quickly supported by two other members and passed by a three-to-two vote. Board President Joseph Stock expressed shock that the board had lost its team orientation and commitment to its goals and objectives. After the meeting, Mr. Stock expressed to the superintendent his worries about the feelings of employees and the community. He blurted out, "Webb has done it again! How do we smooth this over with those who feel betrayed?"

The superintendent and board minority were stunned by the vote and the packed audience divided by joy and anger. Today, Superintendent Chavez has been besieged by angry people. Dr. Reynolds and members of the School Closure Committee are furious. They believe that they have been used by the board and superintendent and that the ultimate decision was known from the start. The local newspaper reporter has expressed anger because he believes that he has been lied to in his frequent interviews with board members and the superintendent. There are threats by West School parents to go to the Civil Liberties Union.

TIME TO PUT YOUR SKILLS TO WORK

Now, as you reflect on the scenario, how would you answer these questions?

1. Who are the key players?
2. What are their political styles?
3. What are their political connections?
4. What are the possible blind spots?
5. What special groups need attention?
6. What political strategies could be used to influence the outcome?
7. What potential ethical dilemmas exist?

Once you have tried your hand at answering these questions, look below to see what we have to say about this scenario. Did you come up with some new insights and ideas?

SCENARIO 1: ANALYSIS

While there are no absolutes in analyzing scenarios, we provide these reflections from our analysis for your consideration.

1. Who Are the Key Players in This Scenario?

The list of key players for this scenario will undoubtedly grow as emotions rise and days pass. As new players are added, the political chemistry will change. Saying that, we can only respond to the scenario in the present. *Superintendent Chavez* will have to work with three key players and a number of others to help facilitate the political response. Key players are *Board Member Elaine Webb, Board President Joseph Stock, and Dr. Bill Reynolds*, who chaired the School Closure Committee.

2. What Are Their Political Styles?

Superintendent Chavez is an adaptor. This is a passive style, blended between self-interest and interest in the organization. She has spoken to none of the School Closure Committee members during the process and has allowed things to just happen with apparent minimal risk to herself. Elaine Webb, as the leader of the board majority, is a challenger. Hardly a diplomat, she understands power and isn't afraid to use it. She got what she wanted. She knows that she has upset people, but she doesn't care. There are indications that this is not a new political style for her.

Board President Joseph Stock's political style is that of a balancer. His first concern is for the culture of the board and the integrity of the district. He feels frustration with the fact that, under his leadership, the board has been divided on this and previous issues. He tries to keep everyone feeling positive.

Dr. Bill Reynolds is a strategist. At personal risk to his respected community standing, he has spent weeks bringing the School Closure Committee together to a unanimous recommendation. He is well networked and influential and is committed to doing what's right to address the pressing needs of the school district.

What about the political styles of the other board members? We don't know from the scenario, but Superintendent Chavez had better quickly analyze them. Is it too late?

3. What Are the Political Connections?

On the face of it, they're pretty obvious, but are they? On one hand, it would appear that Board Member Webb and her allies in this matter are connected, as are Mr. Stock and the other minority member. Are these alliances unique to this scenario, or do they reflect an ongoing relationship? An early analysis by Ellen Chavez might have at least predicted a possibility of the board's decision.

Dr. Reynolds has political connections everywhere. His community activity multiplies those connections. Wherever he goes, people are going to be drawn to him. Integrity is important to him. He is not a happy man right now.

4. What Are the Possible Blind Spots?

Hindsight is always 20/20. Certainly, consideration of blind spots needs to take place on a continuing basis and should have been considered early in the process of school closure. Environmental scanning is a crucial part of becoming a politically intelligent leader. The fact that two board members had a child in one of the schools, and therefore might be biased or susceptible to pressure from neighbors, appears to have been a significant blind spot for the superintendent. An assumption was made that since the board appeared united on the need to close a school and to appoint a committee to make a recommendation on which one, it would be united on accepting the committee recommendation. How well will the board work together after this rough spot?

There are plenty of potential blind spots ahead. What will Dr. Reynolds choose to do? How will the American Civil Liberties Union react to the board's decision? What sources will the newspaper listen to, and what will they choose to report? How should it be managed?

5. What Special Groups Need Attention?

Let's, first of all, deal with the board's right to make the decision. While neither unanimous nor perhaps politically wise, divided votes are a part of democratic decision making. Elected boards are accountable for the decisions they make regardless of the recommendations they receive.

Many, if not all, members of the School Closure Committee will take their lead from Dr. Reynolds as they react to the decision. They invested their time and integrity in the process. Their telephones have been ringing too as the community seeks answers to what happened.

The parents of West Elementary School will want to know why their school was selected after the School Closure Committee had recommended East Elementary School. You can bet that the American Civil Liberties Union and perhaps other interested groups will be part of the discussion. Employee unions and school administrators will also need attention. All will be anxious about how the decision will impact employment and workplace assignments. The superintendent will need to work with the city to address concerns about safety and traffic conditions because of the board's decision.

The newspaper reporter and editorial board will need special attention as they interpret what has taken place and how the change will be implemented. Much of the community has no children in school and will be dependent on the newspaper to assess the wisdom of the district and its provisions for carrying out the decision.

Dr. Chavez will need to be alert to any special groups that are added as the decision becomes well known in the community. Communication with school and community leaders will need to take place to scan for these groups.

6. What Political Strategies Could Be Used to Influence the Outcome?

Realizing that Board Member Elaine Webb is a challenger, the importance of Superintendent Chavez doing her homework could have helped her anticipate political blind spots. Allowing things just to happen only encourages challengers to fill the vacuum. Webb is not only a challenger but a sniper, and meticulous planning helps to outfox them. Regular communication with challengers, even if we don't care for them, is crucial for the politically intelligent leader. You need to know what they're thinking and doing. And you need to communicate with them confidently if you are to gain their respect. Board President Joseph Stock is a balancer. Communication is a key strategy for working with all political types. Assisting him in linking agendas with other board members while looking for win-win solutions may help to rebuild trust among board members and may result in the best possible outcome for the board's decision. Dr. Reynolds is another matter. It would be easy to run from the obligation to deal with this important outsider. Dialogue is absolutely crucial, not only because of his service to the district, but because of his standing in the community. His counsel is still of importance. As a strategist, appealing to superordinate goals could be an effective political strategy with him. Seeking his advice on implementing the board's decision in a way that is good for all the affected students could result in not only improving relationships but in a superior plan.

Dr. Chavez is an adaptor who needs to recognize the importance of analyzing the political styles of herself and of those with whom she must work. This requires the creation of a personal political vision to begin with. Dialogue will be an effective tool in analyzing the styles of others and developing strategies. She must strive to help the board link member agendas and communicate with one another. Her own survival is at stake.

7. What Potential Ethical Dilemmas Are at Stake?

Superintendent Chavez will be receiving many angry and critical calls. She may be tempted to share that she does not support the decision of the board and to describe its internal politics in order to shift responsibility. This would only destroy what is left of the community's trust, as well as its trust of her.

Chavez needs to counsel the board that individual members must focus on the task of planning for an effective school closure rather than demonstrating their dissension in public. Public airing of board discord will only damage the trust of the community and irreparably damage any hope for future mending of relationships.

SCENARIO 2: THE CAT LICENSING LAW

The leader in this scenario, the director of the local Humane Society, wants to put into place a cat licensing law in a local city. He lives in that city, and a number of his board members live and work in that city. He is deeply committed to the issue of spaying and neutering pets to control overpopulation of unwanted and uncared for animals in the community. Although he shies away from the limelight, his dedication to the Humane Society has led him to get involved with community leaders and opinion makers in order to strengthen the support base for the organization. The proliferation of unwanted cats has led him to suggest the cat licensing ordinance, which would require all cat owners to register their pet for $10 a year. The proceeds of this licensure would go to a fund to spay and neuter all pets.

The local city council is in a quandary. They like the Humane Society director, and he has served them well in the past. But there is a very vocal group of cat owners who argue that it is intrusive on their privacy rights to license cats. The mayor is exceptionally analytical and doesn't like political conflict. He is very careful and usually has lots of questions for staff about proposed changes, and he likes to use data to develop careful plans.

The vice mayor is very politically astute and is committed to the city. He is a Rotary and golf buddy of the Humane Society director. He is an assertive risk taker who embraces change. He is also very well networked in the city and enjoys planning tactics that will accomplish city goals. The other council members go with the political winds and like to meet everyone halfway. They prefer to avoid conflict and big risks.

TIME TO PUT YOUR SKILLS TO WORK

Now, as you reflect on the scenario, how would you answer these questions?

1. Who are the key players?
2. What are their political styles?
3. What are their political connections?
4. What are the possible blind spots?
5. What special groups need attention?
6. What political strategies could be used to influence the outcome?
7. What potential ethical dilemmas exist?

Once you have tried your hand at answering these questions, look below to see what we have to say about this scenario. Did you come up with some new insights and ideas?

SCENARIO 2: ANALYSIS

Again, there are no absolutes in analyzing these scenarios. We provide these reflections from our analysis as an opportunity to compare your thoughts with ours.

1. Who Are the Key Players?

The *director* of the Humane Society will have to deal with two major key players: the *mayor* and the *vice mayor*. He will also have to deal with the rest of the *city council members*.

2. What Are Their Political Styles?

The director of the Humane Society is a developer. He is fully committed to the goals of the organization, but he is only interested in a moderate level of political activity. The mayor is a planner. He is risk aversive and slow to change. He will engage in a moderate level of political activity to accomplish his goals, but he likes to see new ideas well planned, with all the potential consequences identified upfront. The vice mayor is a strategist. He is very dedicated to the organization's goals and directions. He understands the need for networking and coalition building, and he is open to new ideas. He has many insights about strategies to use in accomplishing a goal.

The other city council members are balancers. They are risk aversive and prefer stability to big changes. They are well networked and tend to have longevity in their positions.

3. What Are the Political Connections?

The Humane Society director is loosely connected with the whole city council and tightly connected with the vice mayor. The vice mayor is well respected and connected to the other city council members.

4. What Are the Possible Blind Spots?

Where is the city manager on the issue? That is an unknown for the Humane Society director. The city manager is usually a very influential source of information for city council members. The vice mayor and city council members are up for reelection in six months. How will this affect their reelection campaign? Where do dog owners fall on this issue? These unanswered questions could blindside the Humane Society director.

5. What Special Groups Need Attention?

The cat owners need special attention. The director needs to talk with them to understand their concerns and to assess their political determination and strength. The dog owners are another group that should not be overlooked, since they may perceive the council's action as unfair and inequitable to them, if the cat owners are not held to the same standards as they are.

6. What Political Strategies Could Be Used to Influence the Outcome?

Multiple strategies can be helpful here. Forming a committee headed by two of the council members who are open to spay-and-neuter programs would be a good way to get dialogue going and information presented. Some cat owners should be invited to sit on the committee. This will provide an opportunity to learn about each other's interests and to provide more potential for finding a win-win solution. If dog owners are a political force on this issue, they should have representatives on the committee as well. This committee should offer recommendations to the city council.

Knowing the decision makers' agenda is another strategy that could be helpful. The director needs to learn what the hot buttons are of city council members. For example, if reelection is a hot button for those whose term is nearly up, the timing of this item may need to be delayed until after the election in order to be successful. The director should ask the vice mayor about other concerns or interests that council members might have.

The director should build trust by being consistent and honest. He should emphasize mutual interdependence. Including people whom city council members trust on the committee will increase the committee's influence when they make a recommendation.

The director needs to use a clear and simple message that appeals to city council members and the rest of the community, such as "All proceeds will go to the spaying and neutering of all pets." Say no more.

The theory of small wins can be of great assistance here. If the director emphasizes that the program will be implemented on an experimental basis for a year, then the city council can vote to continue or discontinue the program. No strategy is going to completely win over the cat owners, but this approach will give the cat owners a face-saving way out of fighting it.

The director needs to assess when and how hard to push for this new fee. He needs to weigh the pros and cons of moving forward aggressively at this point in time. It's important for him to ask himself if this is the hill he's willing to die on. Winning the battle and losing the war may cost him dearly in his future efforts to advance the goals of his organization. On the other hand, if his organization is committed to a push to spay and neuter pets, and if cat licensing is a good source for funding it, he may need to devote more political capital to this effort. The director must weigh this goal in light of what might be important to the vision of the Humane Society.

7. What Potential Ethical Dilemmas Exist?

There could be a great temptation for the Humane Society director to use his friendship with the vice mayor to attempt to push this new fee through without taking time to involve those affected. He could try to operate under the radar of the cat owners group and pull a power play to achieve his goal without anyone knowing until it's too late. This would undermine the community's trust in both the Humane Society and the city council. On the other hand, backing away from this proposed solution to stewardship of unwanted animals because of risk to his own self-interest would also call his ethics into question.

With sound analysis and strategies, the director can find a solution that is both ethical and politically viable.

SCENARIO 3: THE UNIVERSITY FOUNDATION VS. THE FACULTY

The leader in this scenario is the university president. Promoted from within a few years ago, he is committed to the university's goals, but he is a young family man and is also concerned about keeping his job. In recent years, the need for outside funding has increased to repair, replace, or add technological infrastructure to various colleges within the university. At the same time, university expenses have risen, and finances are stretched thin. He understands that the foundation's methods of fund-raising need to change if he is going to address the university's technology needs. While he has had some concerns about the new foundation chair's style, he has not questioned her methods, because he did not want to appear ungrateful for her hard work.

The new chairperson of the University Foundation Board is very well connected to "high rollers" in the community. She has singlehandedly brought in more money than all of the Foundation Board Members combined, and she enjoys the recognition she gets for her achievements. She is known as a mover and shaker and has been trying to convince the board that they need to have more "say" in what they are funding and should look for donors who are willing to donate money if the university will reciprocate to meet their needs. For example, several large corporations in the area would like to increase enrollment in the school of engineering and build a new program in biomed to improve recruitment opportunities for their jobs.

The most senior member on the foundation board has been slow to agree to some of her strategies. Although he has never been president of the board, he has been instrumental in getting a number of other board members appointed to the board and has coached them in their early years to improve their effectiveness in fund-raising and boardsmanship. In fact, he was responsible for securing an appointment to the foundation board for the new president, and he was on the selection committee for the new university president. However, he disagrees with the new foundation president's approach and believes that the foundation should first and foremost support the goals and needs of the university.

The chair's latest foray into controlling how foundation contributions should be spent is related to the selection of the graduation speaker. Normally, the graduating class nominates speakers, and the president and faculty representatives make the final decision.

The chairperson has selected a very wealthy and well-known CEO whose business profits from U.S. involvement in wartime activity. The chairperson has approached this CEO about making a contribution to the foundation for the school of engineering, which desperately needs new technology. Having him as a graduation speaker would help to bond him with the university and would boost the chairperson's chances of securing a huge donation.

The leader of the Faculty Senate, who has been an antiwar protestor since the 1960s, has informed the university president that the faculty will not attend the graduation ceremonies if this representative of the "military industrial complex" is the speaker. This faculty leader is very well liked by both students and staff. He has been on the faculty a long time and is committed to the ideals of the university, but he prides himself on being an organizer around causes that interest him. He is involved in a number of organizations in town and sits on the museum board with the wife of the senior foundation board member. His connections and strategic skills will help him to deliver on the promise of no attendance.

The foundation board chair's position is that the board will not pay for the speaker unless they determine who it is. And the funding for needed technology is at risk if the proposed speaker is rejected.

You are the university president. What do you do?

TIME TO PUT YOUR SKILLS TO WORK

Now, as you reflect on the scenario, how would you answer these questions?

1. Who are the key players?
2. What are their political styles?
3. What are their political connections?
4. What are the possible blind spots?
5. What special groups need attention?
6. What political strategies could be used to influence the outcome?
7. What potential ethical dilemmas exist?

Once you have tried your hand at answering these questions, look below to see what we have to say about this scenario. Did you come up with some new insights and ideas?

SCENARIO 3: ANALYSIS

Compare your answers to ours to look for key components in your analysis.

1. Who Are the Key Players?

While there are many people involved in this scenario, the *university pres-ident* is really dealing with three key players: the *foundation chair*, the *senior board member*, and the *leader of the Faculty Senate*.

2. What Are Their Political Styles?

The university president is an adaptor. He's passive in his approach and concerned about his self-interest, but he is also committed to the university's goals.

The foundation chair is a challenger. She seeks and is comfortable with a command position. She is decisive and likes to take charge. She is aggressive and politically active. She likes being a mover and shaker and is not apt to involve others in making decisions, unless absolutely necessary.

The senior foundation board member is a developer. He is committed to the university's goals and priorities and is willing to engage in some political activity to make sure they're successful. Although he likes to stay behind the scenes, he coaches and supports others and is respected by them.

The leader of the Faculty Senate is an arranger. He, too, is dedicated to the university's vision, but he is also interested in pursuing his own agenda for change. He is well connected and liked by colleagues, followers, and supervisors. He has the courage to engage in risky activity on behalf of his causes and the organization's needs. He is skilled in strategic action.

3. What Are the Political Connections?

The foundation chair has connections with some of the foundation board and with business leaders. The senior board member is well connected with the foundation board members and the university president. The faculty leader is connected with faculty and students and the senior foundation board member via his wife.

4. What Are Possible Blind Spots?

The university president may not know that the Faculty Senate leader is on the museum board with the wife of the senior foundation board member. He also may not be aware of the level of student support that the Faculty Senate leader has and how they will act on that support. The university president does not know if any of the key players have connections to any of the university board members, who hire and fire presidents. It would be very important to find out whom the foundation chair is connected to.

5. What Special Groups Need Attention?

The university board, the foundation board, the faculty, and the students need attention. The university president needs to do some homework on how they are feeling about this issue.

6. What Political Strategies Could Be Used to Influence the Outcome?

The political styles of all three of the key players the university president has to work with respond well to being included in problem solving and decision making. They also respond well to agenda linking and win-win strategies. Bringing them together to discuss the problem may help to identify the interests that lie behind their positions. Since the foundation chair does not respect passivity, it would be important for the university president to step up to a leadership role with this committee and demonstrate full engagement with them. The university president should capitalize on the relationship that the senior foundation board member has with both the foundation chair and the faculty leader to help moderate their polarized views.

Once they are able to hear each other's real interests, it may be possible to find some common ideas, which would be the basis for linking agendas. The university president would be wise to encourage the creativity of the faculty leader, since his style prizes the "art of the deal," and he would be good at developing solutions to complex problems. Searching for a win-win solution, where everyone's needs get met and no one loses face will be a challenge worth working for. Giving the foundation chair some credit and limelight for resolving the situation would be helpful in maintaining that relationship.

7. What Potential Ethical Dilemmas Exist?

Both the foundation chair and the faculty leader are giving lip service to the organizational vision while advancing their own interests and their own power. The foundation chair's view stems from her belief that the "foundation knows best" how to spend donations from the community. The faculty leader believes the staff knows best. There is a ripening opportunity 'or many factions, each with their parochial view, to engage in a tug of war over resources. The dilemma is, do they pursue their own interests and advance their own power, or do they put the organization first and work together to find a solution that will address student needs and the organization's tenets and vision?

Whatever the outcome of the committee, it is important for all to recognize that the university, of all places, should be a place for free and open expression of ideas and opinions versus suppression of speech and speakers.

Shutting the foundation leaders out of the process for determining potential speakers may send an unintended message. It clearly says that community leaders don't know as much as the faculty, or they must agree with the faculty to be invited in. In the long run, this will not serve the university well, since it depends on the community for fund-raising to give students advantages they could otherwise not afford. Ethical decisions with political consequences!

FINAL THOUGHTS

Analyzing these scenarios can produce a number of lessons to be learned:

1. There are numerous sufficient political strategies that could be used to answer the questions in these scenarios. We have provided some; you have provided others. But there is no single strategy that is the ultimate answer for any of these questions. It is really up to you to select the appropriate ones that work for you as an individual in any situation.

2. The strategies you choose are dependent on (a) the political conditions of the particular situation, (b) your political style, and (c) the political style of others. There may be some strategies that could prove disastrous in certain circumstances or with certain political types. Knowing the difference between those that will work and those that won't is a huge part of political intelligence.

3. Ethical principles should be part of your choice of political strategy. What serves the greater good should be foremost in your mind, not what is in your self-interest. But you should recognize that values sometimes clash, and what is morally right is often difficult to discern. Reflection may be challenging, but reflect you must.

Epilogue

By now, we hope you feel, as we do, that politics are not inherently bad. It only earns a bad name when people misuse it. Politics, in fact, can be ennobling because it gives you the power to lift your people and your organization up—to reach for that vision and those lofty goals that you set together!

As leaders, there were many occasions when differences of opinion were vigorously expressed. There were times when feelings were singed by personal attacks and political blind spots cost us time, energy, and relationships. However, there were also times of incredible highs.

As a superintendent, the elation that spread through the entire district—staff and community—when we used our political strategies to pass a hard-fought bond election is a lasting memory.

As a dean, there was a time when I had the opportunity to allocate scarce resources to start a new, much needed gerontology center on campus. There was a lot of competition for those resources, and the potential for conflict and diminished morale was great. Fortunately, I was blessed by my faculty and given the go-ahead. The center has helped thousands in the years since. I used some of the political know-how I have accrued to gain those resources and use them for a higher purpose.

In another situation, these political strategies made all the difference t a superintendent and an assistant superintendent who were working together to avert a strike with a last-minute negotiated agreement. The politically charged circumstances, with a lot riding on the outcome, increased the importance of skillful handling.

As a councilman, one of the highs came when we were able to pass a hotly contested mobile home rent-control ordinance. Few believed it was possible; the residents were ecstatic, and the ordinance has lasted and worked for the last twenty-two years. Political strategies made it possible to accomplish this.

One of the strategies that we urge you to consider in this book is to celebrate the small wins. This is not only a strategy that draws others to your point of view; it is deeply rewarding for the one who invokes its use. I was always touched to see the notes of praise I wrote posted on teacher bulletin boards many months later, and the "Children First" pins I presented to honor those who advanced our vision worn proudly on lapels for years to come. In this way, we celebrated small wins and used political strategies to tend to the morale of both our followers and ourselves.

These are all political activities and outcomes that were done for the right reasons. Yes, politics can be satisfying and ennobling. It can help the people you serve to be the best that they can be. It can help you deliver the vision that you and they care so much about. This can happen if you use the strategies the right way for the right ends.

RIGHT MEANS

We have provided a set of internal and external strategies for you to use as they are called for. Throughout this book, we have urged you to use the right strategy for each situation. Whether it is to build trust, form a coalition, identify political blind spots, or whatever, we have advised you to match the strategies with the situation.

We have discussed your preferred and default political styles, as well as techniques to use with styles of others. We have empathized with you when you dug yourself a political hole and given you strategies to dig your way out. We have given you a framework to think through your ethical conflicts and manage the political consequences of your decisions. Lastly, we have explored ways to deal with special community groups and associations.

We have suggested the means to help you resolve your most complex problems. It is up to you to use them in a way that works best for you. The means must match the situation and the ends that you are trying to reach.

RIGHT ENDS

We have also called on you to use your will to select good ends for your pursuits. We have urged you to act ethically in your political quests and to keep your values and priorities first and foremost in your mind. In short, we urge you to use these strategies to ennoble the art of leadership.

FINAL CAVEAT

It takes courage to use these strategies for good. Sometimes, self-interest or short-term gain may cause an individual to stray from the high road. It takes courage and willpower to ask ourselves, "How will my actions help the organization and benefit the people therein?" It takes a willingness to face the hard realities of conflict. It takes a mindfulness of ethics, and it often takes a painful self-denial in the application of strategies for the greater good. But this is the road you must take to ensure that your use of politics is truly ennobling, and if you achieve that, what higher praise can you earn?

Appendix

Inventory of Political Styles

Name _____   Date _____

Directions

The Inventory of Political Styles consists of ten major questions presented
in bold print. Each question has a group of nine alternative responses
(a–i). For each question (numbered 1 through 10), you will spread a total
of 10 points across the group of related responses.

You may distribute your points in any way you see fit, allocating from
0 to 10 points on any alternative, but no more than 10 points altogether for
the entire question.

- The highest number of points should be allocated to those alternatives that are most like the way you would respond or feel.
- Zero or the lowest number of points should be allocated to alternatives that are the least like the way you would respond or feel.

Write your points on the line next to the letter code (N–Z) at the end of
each alternative.

Scoring the Responses

When you are finished, record the points for each response on the scoring sheet. Total the points for each letter code and fill in the summary box at the bottom of the scoring sheet.

For Example:

Sample Question 1: Given the opportunity to select an activity for an evening out, I would most likely choose:

a. reading	T	0
b. visiting an art gallery	X	0
c. a jazz concert	Q	0
d. fast food and arcade games	Y	1
e. parachuting out of a plane	V	3
f. riding my Harley	U	4
g. practicing my swing at a driving range	N	0
h. surfing	W	2
i. dinner with friends at my place	Z	0
Total Points		10

INVENTORY OF POLITICAL STYLES: It is important that you answer the questions as realistically as possible. Describe the way you actually tend to behave on the job, rather than how you think someone should behave.

1. When the boss directs that all employees will have to participate in a new training program to improve efficiency and asks for volunteers for the committee to plan it, I tend to:

a. Volunteer to develop the plan myself, since that way it will be done right and fast. Committees just slow things down.	V	_____
b. Let the boss know I like this idea and I'll do my best to help him implement the new plan.	U	_____

c. Tell committee members to go with "proven" solutions rather than somebody's brainchild. N _____

d. Agree to serve on the committee to guide newer staff members in learning how to plan a program that will benefit others. W _____

e. Gather information and prepare an analysis of alternatives that I can share with committee members. T _____

f. Offer to negotiate a deal with the union to schedule training sessions on a shared cost basis, with half the time during the work day and half the time after work hours, to keep costs down and employees happy. Z _____

g. Speak enthusiastically to others about this opportunity to improve the way we do business. Y _____

h. Understand why the boss needs this training program, but worry that making employees participate will ruin morale. I don't want to actually sit on the committee, but I suggest to the committee reps that they should look for some incentives for participation. X _____

i. Volunteer to chair the committee and come up with a collaborative process that will involve all levels of staff in determining how the program will be implemented. Q _____

2. When there is a promotion available in this organization, I tend to:

a. Examine the requirements, wait to see who else applies, look at the person I'd be working for, talk to that person's staff about his style, weigh my changes, consider my current boss's reaction, but probably decide I'm happy enough where I am. N _____

b. Attempt to find out how much competition there is for this job before making my decision to apply, since I don't want to anger my present boss who

doesn't want to see me leave. Fortunately, I have
lots of letters of recommendation from the past in
my file if I decide to apply.   T _____

c. Talk to the personnel director to discuss how my
qualifications align with the organization's vision,
use my networks to learn more about whether my
values and style are a match with those of the new
boss and colleagues, call on my mentor to review
my résumé and help me "bone up" on my
interviewing skills.   Q _____

d. Share what I know about the culture of that
department with others in my network of friends
and associates whom I believe would be a good fit
for the position.   X _____

e. Try to find out if that department is comfortable
with coasting or whether they are ready for some
important changes. If they are, I "call in my chits"
with those I've done favors for and ask them to
write letters of recommendation for me.   V _____

f. Struggle with the decision to apply, since I'm happy
where I am, but would enjoy being a greater part of
moving the organization forward. If I learn that a
colleague is applying, I probably won't apply because
I don't want to destroy the harmony in our relationship.   Y _____

g. Volunteer to sit on the interview committee, since I
have a good understanding of the job, know a lot of
people, and can check references on any of the
applicants I don't know.   Z _____

h. Not even consider applying since I love my job and
the people I work with, and even though the money
would be better, it's not worth giving up the security
and stability of what I have.   U _____

i. Encourage a talented colleague to apply for the job
and help that person with résumés and interviewing
techniques.   W _____

3. When I am a member of a committee to negotiate an agreement on behalf of our organization, I tend to:

a. Lay out our interests. Elicit their interests. Try to find creative ways to connect ours to theirs to come up with a creative solution.   Z _____

b. Look for ways to reduce the level of conflict and acrimony, and try to inject some optimism into the situation.   Y _____

c. Assist the team in reaching our objective, but help others to accept whatever is the final outcome even if we don't reach our objective.   U _____

d. Provide some coaching for our chief negotiator to help him gain insights about the other side's tactics and to help him find win-win solutions.   W _____

e. Although I'm not the chief negotiator, I have good connections with the other side. Therefore, to get things moving, I would hold confidential bargaining talks with the other side.   V _____

f. Try to find out what the other side really wants in order to get this impasse solved. Then try to talk the chief negotiator into giving them as much of what they need as possible, so that morale does not go down the tubes.   X _____

g. Involve both sides in collaborating on creative solutions that support our organizational goal. Look for solutions that benefit both sides. Use strategies that build relationships and trust.   Q _____

h. Take careful notes during negotiations so that we can document who said what and where we had reached tentative agreement.   T _____

i. Keep my opinions to myself and follow the lead of the chief negotiator who gets his direction from the board. In caucuses, suggest that we ask for evidence of the problems.   N _____

4. When communicating with my "reluctant-to-change" boss over a new program I need to propose for our organization, I tend to:

a. Attempt to show him how this program is aligned
   with the organizational vision and also his own goals.   Q _____
b. Provide information about alternatives, but not push
   too hard one way or the other so that I don't
   alienate him.   T _____
c. Talk to him about what could happen if he doesn't
   go ahead with this change that is so important to
   the organization's success.   W _____
d. Share with him what's on the grapevine about this
   program and how popular the idea is with our
   clients, although staff has some reservations about it.
   Ask him what he thinks would make it work.   X _____
e. Provide evidence of where it's worked elsewhere
   and share with him that I normally share his views
   about change, but I've spent a year researching it
   and this one looks like it could be okay.   N _____
f. Have one or two people he trusts and respects join
   me in the presentation to help him see the
   advantages of the change.   Z _____
g. Work around him by first getting the support of his
   supervisor, with whom I play golf twice a month.   V _____
h. Tell him this is really something my staff needs, but
   I'll support whatever he decides.   Y _____
i. Accept that there is little chance for new programs
   and keep doing the best I can with what's available.   U _____

5. A big meeting has been called by the boss to discuss a major problem in the organization as a result of a recent change in delivery systems. Jobs could be at stake. In this meeting, I tend to:

a. Keep quiet but pay close attention.   N _____
b. Indicate my support for necessary changes.   U _____
c. Offer assistance in analyzing the problem and
   generating solutions.   W _____

d. Share anecdotes about how the problem is affecting clients and point out some of the good things that are happening as a result of the change. I look for ways to develop a solution everyone can live with even if it costs more money than we had planned.   X _____

e. When we're on our way out to our cars, I congratulate all of those who spoke up at the meeting.   Y _____

f. Since jobs are at stake, come prepared with good reasons why I should not be regarded as responsible for this situation and be subtle in suggesting possible sources of the problem.   V _____

g. Bring the analysis I did prior to entering the program that shows the downsides I predicted, as a way to help us look for solutions to the problems we are encountering.   T _____

h. Discuss political fallout from the problem and suggest the group brainstorm some strategies that would restore credibility.   Z _____

i. Search for lessons that can be learned from the problem and suggest setting up a committee of stakeholders to plan for future steps that will prevent a recurrence.   Q _____

6. A big committee of which I am a member is responsible for developing an important new program. The committee will be reporting on this program at an upcoming board meeting. In this meeting, I tend to:

a. Provide a copy of all the documents and committee minutes I've taken and give the board alternatives rather than a firm recommendation, since it's their decision.   T _____

b. As a hardworking member of the committee, be there to show support for the board's decision.   U _____

c. Give examples and advise board members as to how this program will contribute to organizational success.   W _____

d. Although I am skeptical of this board's willingness
to accept our committee's proposal, I prepare the
materials for the agenda, showing places where the
program has been successful.   N _____

e. Show how this program relates to the organizational
vision and give credit to the teamwork and creativity
of the committee members.   Q _____

f. Having primed some of the board members ahead
of time to make sure they were receptive to the
proposal, make sure that the speakers include people
the board respects.   Z _____

g. Describe staff and client reaction to this program
concept so far and be prepared with suggestions as
to how we can alleviate possible concerns.   X _____

h. Sit with my committee during the presentation to
give them encouragement but let the others do the
talking.   Y _____

i. Offer to be the main presenter. I enjoy this role, and
it gives me an opportunity to show what I can do,
which doesn't hurt my career goals.   V _____

7. There is an employee uprising against the director of the department where I work. I am the team leader for these employees and report to this director also. A small group of representatives come to me for advice. In this situation, I tend to:

a. Listen to their concerns. Ask them what strategies
they've considered to open up communication
between the staff and the director. Model the
organizational values in my conversation.   Q _____

b. Serve them coffee and cookies, listen to their story,
and be sympathetic, but tell them I'm sorry, but I
have to stay out of it.   Y _____

c. Since I know there's nothing they can do to change
things, let them know that this director is well
connected and that it wouldn't be a good idea to
pursue this.   N _____

d. Tell them we all have to just do our best and ride
   it out.   U _____
e. Since I'm pleased to finally have a mover and shaker
   in the driver's seat, I feel these staff members are
   whiners. I give the director a "heads up" that these
   people are complaining about his leadership style.   V _____
f. Suggest that they ask the director to meet with them
   to listen to their concerns, presented in a calm and
   respectful way. Coach them in how to handle the
   conference for best results.   W _____
g. I'm concerned about morale in the department, so I
   agree to talk to the director for them. I give the
   director some ideas about how to resolve the
   situation by giving the staff some of what they want.   X _____
h. Since I have the trust and respect of both the staff
   and the director, I offer to set up a meeting with
   them and him. I also offer to be there to mediate
   the conversation.   Z _____
i. I help them to look at alternative strategies and
   consequences to determine an appropriate course of
   action. After that, they are on their own to follow up,
   since I've learned not to take on other people's
   problems as my own.   T _____

8. As the new manager of a department, I've just learned that my predecessor has been undermining me with my supervisor, my staff, and my clients. My predecessor has been promoted in the organization and is well thought of. In this situation, I tend to:

a. Look for common interests with my predecessor
   and try to find a common project to work on so that
   we are interdependent for success in our
   respective roles.   Z _____
b. Seek the advice of my mentor. Brainstorm
   alternatives. Keep careful records of incidents,
   correspondence, e-mail messages with everyone as
   a precaution.   T _____

c. Do my job as well as I can and let my work speak
for itself.   U _____

d. Avoid getting involved in the politics and "go to the
balcony" to stay calm, objective, and avoid
overreacting. I stay optimistic that everything will
work out.   Y _____

e. Feel I realistically have no chance of surviving this.
I start preparing for my departure and looking for
work elsewhere.   N _____

f. Build positive relationships and networks around
common goals and interests with the people in my
department and my clients, as well as the executive
staff, so that they are less likely to believe false stories.   Q _____

g. Fight fire with fire by using the same tactics to let
people know how he is maligning me and to seek
their help in discrediting his actions with the
executive staff.   V _____

h. Keep informal communication lines open with all
parties to learn what's going on and to set the
record straight with my staff and clients. I work
on learning more about the culture and the key
opinion makers so that I can avoid the sacred cows
as I move forward.   X _____

i. Look for a win-win alternative with my predecessor.
Tell those who are concerned about the "politics"
that these things are natural during times of
organizational change and they should just avoid
taking sides.   W _____

9. Clients are very upset with some changes that have been made in the service structure. Although the changes have been ordered by the CEO, the staff is blaming me for problems and lack of follow-through on promises. In this situation, I tend to:

a. Slow down. I will study the problem and avoid
taking more risks.   N _____

b. Tell them I'm just following the CEO's direction,
and I completely understand their concerns.   U _____

c. Attend a meeting with them but get my supervisor, who has more experience, to facilitate the meeting and do the talking so that I can listen and reflect. I really support both the CEO and the staff.   Y _____

d. See this as a natural human reaction to change and accept their input. Provide honest information about the reasons the changes were put in place and ask for their patience in allowing me to implement necessary changes in my operation. Tell them I'll help them develop their skills in the new program.   W _____

e. Tell them changes need to take place if this organization is going to stay afloat. Let them know their jobs are at stake if we do not turn the operation around. After all, I'm there to cut losses, not win popularity contests.   V _____

f. Meet with them to listen to their concerns. Develop a plan to address their issues and still maintain the integrity of the organizational goals. Collaborate on next steps.   Q _____

g. Present all my documentation and records clarifying the situation and demonstrating that their concerns, in fact, have no basis. Share with them my action plan for implementing the change.   T _____

h. Tell them that you believe things will get better if they just give the new system a chance. Share stories of other places in the organization where it's been well received, to build optimism. Ask them what would make them feel more comfortable with the change.   X _____

i. Try to discover what their real interests are and look for ways to address these interests and the organization's needs as well. Try to link my agenda with theirs to achieve a mutually acceptable solution.   Z _____

10. I work for someone who is incompetent and impulsive. He seems to be a favorite with the upper levels of administration but does not have a good relationship with most of his staff because when things go

wrong, he blames them. He has given me an assignment that has the potential for blowing up politically. In this situation, I tend to:

a. Try to find out what the boss really needs and meet
   him halfway by suggesting some solutions that will
   work for him and save me from taking a risk that
   could blow up.   X _____

b. Stand my ground and let him know that I think this
   is a bad idea and that unless he withdraws the
   assignment, I will go to the CEO to let her know
   about the potential consequences.   V _____

c. Consider alternative approaches that could provide
   a safer route to the goal. Recognize that I am
   powerless to avoid this assignment and prepare for
   the political explosion, for which I will probably
   get blamed.   N _____

d. Get a few people the boss trusts to help me explain
   to him the potential consequences of this assignment
   and develop creative solutions that meet his interests
   and avoid the political fallout.   Q _____

e. Use honesty and compassion in dealing with him by
   pointing out the reasons for the likely failure of this
   project and by diplomatically showing him the
   potential impact on his own job security.   Z _____

f. Support his decision, but plan my defense when it
   blows up.   T _____

g. Accept his direction, and hope for the best possible
   outcome.   U _____

h. Talk to him about my prediction of a political
   explosion, and give him some coaching about
   involving staff in decisions before he makes major
   policy changes.   W _____

i. Let staff know that we have to go forward with this
   new project, and I would appreciate their support
   and help. I would be optimistic with them about
   getting through it.   Y _____

SCORING SHEET

Scoring the Responses

When you are finished, record the points for each response on the scoring sheet. Total the points for each letter code. Then fill in the summary box at the bottom of the scoring sheet.

Question	1	2	3	4	5	6	7	8	9	10	Total
N											
Q											
T											
U											
V											
W											
X											
Y											
Z											
Total											

Summary Boxes

Highest Score	Letter	Style

Lowest Score	Letter	Style

Answer Key

Code	Political Style
N	Analyst
Q	Strategist
T	Planner
U	Adaptor
V	Challenger
W	Developer
X	Balancer
Y	Supporter
Z	Arranger

References

The American heritage dictionary (10th edition). (2001). Boston: Houghton Mifflin Co.

Blake, R. R., and Mouton, J. S. (1964). *The managerial grid*. Houston: Gulf Publishing Company.

Bolman, L. G., and Deal, T. E. (1991). *Reframing organizations: Artistry, choice and leadership*. San Francisco: Jossey-Bass.

Bradberry, T., and Greaves, J. (2005). *The emotional intelligence quick book*. New York: Simon & Schuster.

Brandon, R., and Seldman, M. (2004). *Survival of the savvy: High-integrity political tactics for career and company success*. New York: Free Press.

Carson, R. (2003). *Taming your gremlin*. New York: Harper Collins Publishers.

Coffin, C. (Ed.). (2001). *Complete poetry and selected prose of John Donne*. New York: Modern Library.

Collins, J. (2001). *Good to great*. New York: Harper Collins Publishers.

Covey, S. R. (1989). *Seven habits of highly effective people*. New York: Simon & Schuster.

Covey, S. R. (1991). *Principle-centered leadership*. New York: Summit Books.

De Luca, J. (1999). *Political savvy*. Berwyn, PA: EBG Publications.

Deutch, M. (1949). A theory of cooperation and competition. *Human Relations*, 2, 129–152.

Dobel, J. P. (1998). Political prudence and the ethics of leadership. *Public Administration Review*, 58 (1), 74–81.

Ellinor, L., and Gerard, G. (1998). *Dialogue*. New York: John Wiley & Sons.

Fisher, R., and Ury, W. (1988). *Getting to yes: Negotiating agreement without giving in*. New York: Penguin Books.

165

French, J. R. P., and Raven, B. (1959). The bases of power. In D. Cartwright, *Studies of social power* (pp. 150–167). Ann Arbor: Institute for Social Research.

Gladwell, M. (2005). *Blink*. New York: Little, Brown & Company.

Goleman, D., Boyatzis, R., and McKee, A. (2002). *Primal leadership: Realizing the power of emotional intelligence*. Boston: Harvard Business School Publishing.

Greenleaf, R. K. (1977). *Servant leadership*. New York: Paulist Press.

Harvey, T. R. (1979). Transaction in the change process. In J. Jones and W. Pfeiffer, eds., *The 1979 annual handbook for group facilitators* (p. 64). San Diego: University Associates.

Harvey, T., and Drolet, B. (2004). *Building teams, building people*. Lanham, MD: Scarecrow Press.

Harvey, T., Bearley, W., and Corkrum, S. (2001). *The practical decision maker*. Lanham, MD: Scarecrow Press.

Heifetz, R., and Linsky, M. (2002). *Leadership on the line*. Cambridge: Harvard Business School Press.

Josephson, M. (2005). *Making ethical decisions: The six pillars of character*. Retrieved June 14, 2005, from http://www.josephsoninstitute.org/MED/MED-2sixpillars.html.

Kanter, R. M. (2004). *Confidence: How winning streaks and losing streaks begin and end*. New York: Crown Business.

Lustberg, A. (1984). *Winning at confrontation*. Washington, D.C.: U.S. Chamber of Commerce.

Marcic, D. (n.d.). *Hospitable to the human spirit: An imperative for organizations*. Retrieved October 17, 2006, from http://bbfa.org/resources/articles/marcic-hospitabletospirit.pdf.

McDonald, G., and Nijhof, A. (1999). Beyond codes of ethics: An integrated framework for stimulation of morally responsible behavior in organizations. *Leadership & Organizational Development Journal, 20* (3), 133–146.

Nutt, P. (1960). *Making tough decisions*. San Francisco: Jossey-Bass.

Patterson, K., Grenny, J., McMillan, R., and Switzer, A. (2002). *Crucial conversations: Tools for talking when stakes are high*. New York: McGraw-Hill.

Pfeffer, J. (1981). *Power in organizations*. Marshfield, MA: Putnam.

Reardon, K. K. (2001). *The secret handshake*. New York: Currency Books.

Sanders, I. (1998). *Strategic thinking and the new science*. New York: Free Press.

Shapiro, J. P., and Stefkovich, J. A. (2001). *Ethical leadership and decision making in education: Applying theoretical perspectives to complex dilemmas*. Mahwah, NJ: Lawrence Erlbaum Associates.

Silberman, M., and Hansburg, F. (2000). *PeopleSmart*. San Francisco: Berrett-Koehler Publishers.

Spitzer, E. (2005). My golden rule. *Business 2.0*, 11, 114.

Stodgil, R. M. (1974). *Handbook of leadership*. New York: Free Press.

Ursiny, T. (2003). *The coward's guide to conflict*. Naperville: Sourcebooks.

Ury, W. (1993). *Getting past no*. New York: Penguin Books.

Index

About the Authors

Patricia Clark White has been superintendent of three award-winning California school districts, a national and international consultant and presenter, and an executive coach to leaders dealing with political issues. She has been associated with the University of La Verne Organizational Leadership Department for over twenty years and is currently an organizational development consultant.

Thomas R. Harvey is a professor of organizational leadership in the doctoral program at the University of La Verne. He has been the dean of the School of Organizational Management and the chairman of the Department of Educational Management for fourteen years and is the author of several books including *Checklist for Change*; *The Practical Decision Maker*; *Building Teams, Building People*; and *The Soul of Leadership*.

Lawrence Kemper is a professor of organizational leadership at the University of La Verne. Prior to joining the university, he served a twenty-one-year career as superintendent of schools of four school districts. He is a past president of the Association of California School Administrators and has been a city planning commission member.

Printed in Great Britain
by Amazon.co.uk, Ltd.,
Marston Gate.